The Cash-Strapped Person's Guide to Thriving in the Digital Age

The Cash-Strapped Person's Guide to Thriving in the Digital Age

Written, Drawn, and Photographed by

Kimberly Keyes

Cover Art by Kimberly Keyes

You Can Access Technology on a Low Budget!

Get a computer without going into debt!

Get legal virus-free software for free or low-cost!

Get training without losing your shirt!

Get software for your kids without draining your wallet!

Access the Internet for free for low-cost!

Make friends and express yourself online for free!

Look for the perfect job without spending a dime!

Live the digital lifestyle to the fullest on a budget!

Plus a special free surprise at the end of this book!

Dedication

I dedicated this book to my family and friends who have stuck by me when I went through two hip surgeries, a divorce, and near-destitution in rapid succession.

Table of Contents

Acknowledgements 13

In the Beginning… 15

Introduction 16

Why I Wrote This Book 19

About the Terminology Used in This Book 23

Hardware Alternatives 26

How to Use a Computer Without Owning a Computer 27

How to Use a Smartphone Like a Regular Computer 29

Obtaining a Computer on a Very Limited Budget: Buy Used 34

Obtaining a Computer on a Very Limited Budget: Buy a Cheap New Computer 38

How to Print Documents If You Don't Own a Printer 40

How to Scan Documents If You Don't Own a Scanner 41

The Internet Zone   42

How to Access the Internet on a Very Limited Budget 43

How to Access the Internet Using Your Smartphone as a Hotspot for Your Computer 46

Build Your Own Internet Access That Benefits Your Community 47

Free Alternatives to Software Produced by Big Corporations 49

Free Alternatives to Microsoft Office 50

Free and Not-So-Free Alternatives to Microsoft Windows 52

Free Alternatives to Adobe Creative Cloud 54

Free Alternatives to Adobe Photoshop 54

Free Alternatives to Adobe Illustrator 56

Free Alternatives to Adobe Flash and AfterEffects 57

Free Alternatives to Adobe Fuse 58

Free Alternatives to Adobe Connect 58

Free Alternatives to Adobe InDesign 59

Free Alternatives to Adobe Dreamweaver 59

Free Alternatives to Adobe Fonts 60

Free Elements to Use in Your Websites, Blogs, Desktop
Publishing, Multimedia Presentations, and Other Creative
Projects 61

Free Photos and Clip Art 62

Free Apps for Podcasting, Screencasting, Videomaking, and
Musicmaking 63

Free Music and Sound Clips For Your Projects 67

Free Survey Tools 68

Free Mailing List Software 69

Free Computer Compilers and Editors for Aspiring

Programmers and Coders 70

Creating Blogs and Websites For Free 74

Free Blogs 75

Free Web Server Spaces 79

Free For Kids 83

The Over 50 Zone 88

How to Obtain Further Education and Training Online Without Losing Your Shirt 91

Free Skills Training Classes 94

Free Foreign Language Classes 96

The Job Zone 98

Free Online Job Search Resources 99

The Gig Economy 105

For Entrepreneurs Only 112

Bitcoin and Other Cryptocurrencies: Don't Believe the Hype 114

Solid and Inrupt: Believe the Hype 119

Accessing the Digital Leisure Lifestyle For Free 124

Social Media 125

Free Online Entertainment 130

Free Recipes Online 132

Free eBooks 133

Free Sites For Online Dating or Just Meeting New People in General 135

Exploring Your Spirituality 137

Support Your Local Library and STEM/STEAM Makerspace 140

Protecting Yourself Legally Without Spending Tons of Money on Legal Fees 143

Other Free Resources 148

In Conclusion 150

A Special Treat For Those Who Have Read This Book 152

About the Author 160

Acknowledgments

I have to thank my friend Phil Shapiro for being a walking treasure trove of information on how to find free computers and other software. His biggest cause is to bridge the digital divide between the haves and have nots while building communities in the process. Years ago he was the subject of this Washington Post article that's definitely worth reading (http://www.his.com/~pshapiro/themanwhogives2.pdf).

I want to thank the tireless volunteers at the Greenbelt Makerspace (https://www.make125.org) for giving me an education on the concept of a makerspace and the maker movement in general. Makerspaces are a great resource for learning about some of the alternative projects being built that could possibly help society in general.

I want to acknowledge Paint Branch Unitarian Universalist Church in Adelphi, Maryland (http://www.pbuuc.org) for inspiring me to write that chapter on how to defend yourself legally despite tight finances. I attended a service at that church on Sunday, September 16, 2018 titled "History Has Its Eyes on Us." It included a discussion on Timothy Snyder's book *On Tyranny* and it gave me the idea of writing that chapter since civil liberties in the United States are increasingly being threatened on a regular basis and it could impact computers and technology in general.

I want to thank my parents, Johanne Keyes and the late John Keyes, for giving me a chance to even go to college in the first place. At long last I found a use for that journalism degree that they had shelled out a lot of money for all those years ago.

I want to thank my family and friends for being supportive to me over the years and not giving up on me when times got tough for me.

I also want to thank all of the companies, groups, and

individuals that continue to come out with free or low cost hardware and software even though they lack the financial resources of a Microsoft or Adobe. They continue with their task of providing affordable technology for the masses without any recognition or glory, which is amazing.

In the Beginning...

Introduction

First of all I want to say that there is no shame in being a cash-strapped poor or low income person. You are not a bad person for not having a lot of money in your bank account and even less money in your wallet. You may have internalized the idea of being poor equals being lazy and irresponsible, which is a negative stereotype that have been prevalent in this society ever since Ronald Reagan's mythical Welfare Queen (the woman who doesn't work yet collects welfare while driving Cadillacs, wearing fur coats, and eating a steady diet of surf and turf or something like that). This attitude has resulted in this awful fusion of Calvinist Christianity, Ayn Rand's Objectivism, and Social Darwinism that is currently prevalent in society, which states that if you're low income, it's your fault, it's God's will, it's God's punishment for not being holy enough, and you're not tough enough since only the strongest survives so you're totally worthless.

In reality there are many reasons why one becomes low income and it's frequently due to circumstances beyond that person's control, such as being a single parent who is getting little or no child support from the other parent, dealing with physical or mental health issues, being unable to find a job due to sexism/racism/homophobia/transphobia/age discrimination, etc.

What's even more mind-blowing is that the standards for being low income vary from place to place and it's mainly due to the cost of living. Usually a person is considered to be doing well if he/she has an income of $100,000 per year. That's not the case in Silicon Valley, where $100,000 is considered to be low income! (https://www.mercurynews.com/2017/04/22/in-costly-bay-area-even-six-figure-salaries-are-considered-low-income/)

You are at a moment of transforming your own life and buying this book is a major first step in doing something positive that could change your life for the better. Don't let other people tell you that you won't make it or that you'll always be poor so don't even bother trying. In fact, you need to distance yourself from anyone who's telling you that as much as you possibly can. (I know it can be daunting challenge if the naysayer is a member of your own family or someone at work—in that situation you should just not bother telling that person about what you are trying to do.) It's a brave new world out there and you deserve to be part of it as a full-functioning member of society who is treated with basic respect and common decency.

In 1971 the late radical Yippie leader Abbie Hoffman published a tome with this provocative title: *Steal This Book*. It was a practical guide to living without working the typical corporate 9-to-5 jobs that were prevalent in that era. While the book contained incendiary language (such as referring to police officers as "pigs"), it also included practical tips—some of which were illegal—on how to obtain food, clothing, furniture, housing, medical care, entertainment, and other things for free or low cost. I once perused a reprint of *Steal This Book* in a bookstore back in the early 2000s. While most of the information in the book had become dated by then (due mainly to changing technology and regulations), I understood why people of a certain age revered this book because it had practical advice for those who wanted to live and thrive in a lifestyle that was different from what was then-promoted as the mainstream American dream lifestyle at the time (which consisted of living in a house in the suburbs with a spouse, two kids, and maybe even a pet or two while owning a car in order to commute to and from a corporate 9-to-5 job in the city from Monday-Friday).

If you want to learn more, a free PDF version of *Steal This Book* is now available at the Internet Archive for reading online or downloading to your computer or smartphone to be read later. It's like stealing this book, except that it's perfectly legal to do so. https://archive.org/details/pdfy-TNIDHryRIk4DXKAU

Times have definitely changed since Steal This Book was published. Technology has opened up for more and more people, which led to many of them thriving in careers that simply didn't exist 20, 30, or even 40 years ago (such as social media marketing manager). Yet access to such technology has led to further income inequality because it's a well-known fact that the more money you have, the more likely you'll be able to access the latest computer with high-end software, the fastest Internet connection ISP package, and top-of-the-line computer peripherals (such as a 3D printer). If you're a cash-strapped person, access to the latest and greatest technology seems pretty daunting because you need to worry about other things like paying rent or utilities so you won't end up living on the streets or living in a place with no electricity or running water.

What's more, it has gotten to the point where access to technology is no longer optional for most people. While you can still get by in society despite opting not to read books or newspapers, watch television, or listen to the radio, it's much harder to get by if you don't have a computer or mobile device. Many jobs needing to hire additional people these days not only require that you have basic computer knowledge but they also require that you apply online. (And that includes retail and fast food jobs that don't really require much computer work.) More stores are using coupons that can only be obtained through certain smartphone apps. More schools are using technology for things like posting a copy of an upcoming lesson plan online or conferring with parents via email about their child's grades.

While being able to afford technology is daunting to a cash-strapped person, it's not impossible. This book is intended as a practical guide to being able to obtain a computer or mobile device—along with software, peripherals, and Internet access—without breaking your budget or having to file for bankruptcy. While *Steal This Book* mentioned obtaining certain things using illegal methods, this book focuses exclusively on obtaining access to technology the legal way. In other words, if you're interested in obtaining an illegal pirated counterfeit copy of Microsoft Office or learning how to successfully shoplift a smartphone or computer from a store, this is NOT the book for you.

This book assumes that you already have a basic understanding of computers, smartphones, and the Internet (such as knowing what a web browser is or knowing the basic difference between Microsoft Word and Adobe Photoshop or knowing how to turn on WiFi and/or Bluetooth on your computer or smartphone). If you know absolutely nothing about computers or technology, I would advise you to go to your local public library or community center because they generally have referrals to basic introductory computer classes that are either free or very low-priced. You can also go online and take a basic introduction class called "What is a Computer?" for free through GCF Learn Free. (https://edu.gcfglobal.org/en/computerbasics/what-is-a-computer/1/)

Why I Wrote This Book

Before I go any further, I just want to write a few words on what motivated me to write this book. The ability to access affordable technology has affected me on a personal level. I married to a man who had a stable well-paying job at NASA. While I worked at a variety of low-paying clerical jobs, my husband's salary more than made up for my low income. Even then we had to watch our money as we decided whether to get a computer and, if so, which brand along with being able to figure out what software we could afford.

At one point I took the entrepreneurial route and I started selling my handcrafted items at various local street festivals in the spring and fall. While I never made a lot of money, I made enough to be able to afford an occasional splurge, such as eating out at a French restaurant that we both loved.

But then, one-by-one, my situation changed drastically. The economic meltdown of 2008 led to declining sales of my handcrafted items at various shows and it got to the point where I was barely breaking even at many of these shows. I had health issues that resulted in hip surgery in 2008 and again in 2011. In late 2011, just three months after my second hip surgery and three days after Christmas, my husband came home from work, announced that he was leaving, then bolted out the door before I could say anything.

I suddenly found myself divorced with few job prospects. I tried getting clerical work using the methods that had previously worked for me—going to temp agencies—only to find out that the temp agencies didn't have work available for me. I found work on my own but they all turned out to be short-lived gigs that didn't pay well. In 2016 I walked off the job at a startup after a few weeks because the owner/founder didn't pay me. I went back to the temp agencies but they didn't have jobs. I went to my state's American Jobs Center where I attended a variety of workshops and networking events that provided tips on finding a job but the only thing that materialized for me as a result was serving a two-night stint as an extra at a taping of a television special that was hosted by personal financial expert Ric Edelman.

I never intended to go for two years without working. I did everything possible to land a new job but to no avail. My ex-husband had been paying me monthly alimony. The amount was small but I was able to pay most of my important bills (such as utilities) yet it didn't leave much financial room for purchases like a new computer or smartphone. Unlike the old days, when a woman would get alimony from her ex-husband either for the rest of her life or until she remarried (whichever came first), alimony these days only lasts a maximum of five years. I was frantically searching for a job where I can support myself before the alimony expired but that didn't happen. In fact, I didn't get my latest gigs doing some freelance administrative work and teaching the elderly how to use their smartphones until a couple of months after the alimony checks stopped coming.

In the meantime I had to turn to other methods of finance in order to be able to afford technology. When my old smartphone died, I used a credit card to purchase a new one (a Droid Ultra) from the Verizon store. By the time that phone was on its last legs a few years later, I grew tired of Verizon jacking up my monthly phone rate to a whopping $125 per month. I had a kind friend give me a used Samsung Galaxy J3 phone he obtained through someone else who had recently upgraded his phone. I switched to Consumer Cellular as the carrier. I ordered just the Mini SD card, which I then installed in that Samsung phone with a little help from a few volunteers at the local makerspace where I asked for help in doing this.

When my hard drive on my five-year-old MacBook (which my husband purchased for me a few years before he left me) finally collapsed beyond all repair, I was already maxed out on my credit card so I had to get my mother to buy me a new MacBook.

When I was still married my husband purchased the Adobe Creative Suite 4 package for me, where I practiced Photoshop, InDesign, Dreamweaver, and Flash on a regular basis. When Adobe decided to switch to an online monthly subscription for its software, I was divorced by then so I had to continue making do with the outdated Creative Suite 4 software while also taking a look at free open source alternatives to Adobe (such as GIMP and Inkscape). I still use a 15-year-old Canon MX860 printer/scanner/copier/fax because 1) it still works and 2) buying a newer printer/scanner/copier/fax is not financially feasible for me at the moment.

Over time I learned that a non-profit makerspace was opening in my neighborhood, known as the Greenbelt Makerspace, which turned out to be a great resource. It was through the Greenbelt Makerspace that I have access to equipment which I currently cannot afford to purchase for myself, such as a 3D printer. (I will go into the concept of makerspaces later in this book.) I began going to meet-ups throughout the Washington, DC metro area where I met people who are not only into bridging the digital divide but they were valuable resources in terms of knowing where to buy a certain computer without paying thousands of dollars or what are some solid free open source alternatives to Microsoft Office.

Not too long ago I had a job interview with a shop that specializes in creating custom one-of-a-kind t-shirts and accessories (such as hats and bags), especially for groups and events (such as a Little League softball team or a company picnic). The woman who interviewed me saw that I mentioned Inkscape on my resume as among the skills I had and she asked me what it was. I told her that Inkscape is a vector graphics program that is the free open source alternative to Adobe Illustrator. Her eyes lit up when I mentioned the words "free alternative to Adobe Illustrator." She probed further so I told her about how one could legally obtain Inkscape for free and start creating vector graphics that can export files that are compatible with Adobe Illustrator and other popular graphics programs without worrying about taking out a subscription. She immediately said, "I need to look into this because I'm getting tired of paying Adobe for that subscription each month."

I ultimately didn't get the job so I have no idea whether her shop actually made the switch to Inkscape or if she chose to keep on subscribing to Adobe. But my experience at that job interview had me thinking that there has to be some way of getting the word out to the general public, especially businesses, that there are free software alternatives to the ones from the big corporations that can produce files that are compatible with the more expensive and popular software. In recent years, many of the free software have performed just as well or even superior to the giant corporation-produced software. Sure one can spend a few hours doing Google searches on "alternatives to [COMPUTER OR SOFTWARE PACKAGE]" but that can be time-consuming and not everyone has the luxury to spend time doing that.

So I wrote this book in an effort to pass on what I have learned from the people I've met in the years since my marriage ended so you, too, can access digital technology while living on a very tight budget.

About the Terminology Used in This Book

I will frequently refer to certain software and operating systems as being "free" or "free open source." There's a technical difference between the two but the bottom line is that, for your purposes, the software is legally free for you to download and it's virus-free as well. For the vast majority of you who are reading this, you really don't need to concern yourself with whether a certain free software is open source or not.

For those of you who are curious, here's a brief explanation of the difference between "free" and "free open source."

Free software is software that is given away for free. However, once you obtain the software, you cannot alter the underlying code in any way.

Free open source software is also software that is given away for free. The reason why it's called "open source" is because, if you are the type of person who loves to code and want to tweak the underlying code behind the software, you can do so. What you have to do is download the original source code from one of the following sites:

GitHub https://github.com

GitLab https://about.gitlab.com

Bitbucket https://bitbucket.org/

SourceForge https://sourceforge.net

Launchpad https://launchpad.net

Once you download the source code, you can just play around with it. If you discover something that could improve the software, you are expected to upload your tweaked code on GitHub/GitLab/Bitbucket/SourceForge/Launchpad.

Here is what it means on a practical level. Two of the alternatives to Adobe Photoshop that are mentioned later in this book are GIMP and Autodesk SketchBook. Both are bitmap graphic programs and both are available for free. The main difference is that GIMP is open source and Autodesk SketchBook is not.

What it means is that if you want to tweak the coding behind GIMP, you can go to GitHub, GitLab, Bitbucket, SourceForge, or Launchpad download the original source code for GIMP, and play around with it. If you discover something that makes GIMP easier to use, you can upload it back to GitHub/GitLab/Bitbucket/SourceForge/Launchpad.

In contrast, even though Autodesk SketchBook is free to download, you can not download the original source code and make your own tweaks with it because Autodesk will not permit it. You are permitted only to download the software and use it for your graphic projects—not alter the underlying code of the software itself.

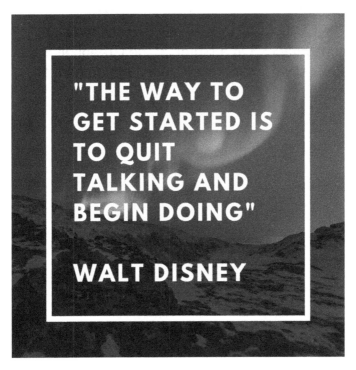

Hardware Alternatives

Oranges attached to a laptop at the Greenbelt Spring Maker Festival in Greenbelt, Maryland on April 14, 2018.

How to Use a Computer Without Owning a Computer

Let's say you're in a situation where you really need to use a computer but you currently don't own one because you can't afford to buy one. Here are a few alternatives you can pursue.

Do you have a job where you have access to a computer with Internet access? If so, that's one option. If you decide on this method, keep in mind that you'll need to strike a balance between doing your own work and doing the work that your company hired you to do because if your boss catches you spending too much time on your own work, there could be very serious consequences.

On top of it, some companies have strict rules on using office equipment for personal use and violating those rules could lead to a lot of consequences ranging from a reprimand to a demotion to even being terminated. I would strongly advise you to look at your company's employee handbook regarding its policies on computer usage for personal reasons before you start doing this.

Plus there are instances where using your work computer might not even be feasible. Let's say your company allows you to use the computer for personal use but only before 9 a.m. or after 5 p.m. If you're single and childless, it would be no big deal for you to come in to work early or stay after work to do your personal computing. But if you happen to be married and/or have children or you have a second job that you work at a few nights a week, this option would not work at all.

There are other alternatives to secretly doing your own computer work with your workplace computer. Most public libraries these days have computers that patrons can use for free. The only requirement is that you must sign up for a library card. Otherwise you can use the library computers for surfing the Internet or typing and printing a document or playing a video game or doing online research, etc. But there are drawbacks as well. You might not live within walking distance to a library, you might not have a car, and the library in question might not be on any bus routes. Even if you have no problem getting to a library, getting access to a computer may be difficult because so many people use the computers that you can't even find an empty computer to sit at. A certain library's computer might not have the software you need installed due to tight budget constraints. Your time at the computer might be limited due to the huge amount of people needing to use those computers. You also might have a job with a schedule where you have to be at work at the same time that the library is open and the library is closed at other times when you're not working.

Some of the larger houses of worship (especially the ones with 1,000 or more members) may have a computer room or two. Some may reserve their computers to church members only while others may offer access to the general public regardless if they are members or not as part of their social justice ministry. If you know of such a house of worship, that may be another computer source for you.

In recent years there have been more and more makerspaces that have been opening in many communities nationwide. A makerspace is a community-operated workspace where people gather to make things and share tips among each other. It's not unusual to see two or more people in a makerspace decide to collaborate together on a project. A typical makerspace will have computers available to use along with printers (including both traditional paper printers and the newer 3D printers), drawing tablets, and other devices. Fees for using a makerspace vary from makerspace to makerspace.

Some makerspaces charge a monthly or annual membership fee and they make their computers and other equipment available to members only while others make some of their facilities available for free while charging a free for special programs (such as summer tech camps for children). While a makerspace is still a relatively new concept, they have been gaining ground in recent years with more and more such facilities opening all the time. You can look for the nearest makerspace in your area by asking various people (such as neighbors, friends, relatives, or co-workers) or doing a quick Google search on "makerspace near me" (without the quotation marks).

There's also the smartphone option. Many low-income people already use their smartphone as their primary computer. I'll go into how this is possible in the next section.

How to Use a Smartphone Like a Regular Computer

Trying to borrow a computer from your job, public library, house of worship, or makerspace is a good solution but even that has limits. You can't store your own files on the computer since it belongs to someone else and other people use it. Unless you remember to bring a USB flash drive with you when you use someone else's computer, you won't have a copy of whatever file you created during your computer session. On top of it, borrowing someone else's computer can become a major drag after a while.

You'll eventually get to the point where you would like to have something to call your very own. One where you can keep your files on the hard disk without having to deal with carrying a USB flash drive to store them.

One way to do so is to use your smartphone. Many low income people already use their smartphone as their primary computer because it's cheaper than buying a new laptop or desktop computer. The best way to obtain a smartphone is through a mobile carrier. Many carriers offer package deals where you get a smartphone at a reduced cost. You'll definitely need to shop around since these package deals vary from carrier to carrier and they may change over time. I would recommend going to the public library and reading back issues of Consumer Reports that deal with smartphones (you can ask your librarian for help on that one) in order to decide for yourself which smartphone and carrier is best for you at the best cost. I would also recommend asking your friends, family, and co-workers about what smartphones and carriers they use. It's a good idea to do your homework before you make a purchasing decision.

Many smartphones come with web browsers so one can surf the Internet. Many sites (such as Buzzfeed, Facebook, and YouTube) offer their own dedicated apps so one can go directly to that site without having to use a web browser. One can check email through a smartphone. Many smartphones also come with work productivity software (such as Google Docs for the Droid, which is a word processor software) and drivers that will allow the smartphone to connect wirelessly with a printer in order to print something.

There are limitations, such as having to deal with viewing through a small screen and typing on a small onscreen keyboard using just one or two fingers. However, there is a workaround for using that tiny onscreen keyboard. You can purchase a used wireless Bluetooth keyboard through eBay or Craigslist. You can also purchase a new wireless Bluetooth keyboard with prices starting at $15. I recommend shopping around to get the best bargain.

Once you get your wireless keyboard, there are a few simple things you'll need to do in order to get it to work directly with your smartphone. First, turn your Bluetooth keyboard on. (You may need to make sure that you have fresh batteries installed before you do this.) Then go to your smartphone and open the Settings app (it's usually located among the apps section of your phone—if you can't find it, ask a friend, neighbor, local librarian, or tech-savvy teen to find it for you). Next look for the "Bluetooth" label. Touch the Bluetooth label then slide a lever in order to turn it on. Now wait for the phone to recognize the keyboard, which generally takes about a minute or two. (It will let you know when it sees the keyboard.) You can now start typing on your phone with the Bluetooth keyboard like you would with a regular computer.

You may wonder about using a mouse with this setup. In this situation your finger is the mouse because your smartphone has a touch screen. All you have to do is use your finger, select the area where you want to start typing, then switch to your Bluetooth keyboard and start typing.

There are plenty of productivity apps that you can download from the App Store or Google Play including word processors, spreadsheets, presentation software, and more. These apps are another reason why you should use a Bluetooth keyboard if you intend to do a lot of typing.

At this point the big challenge is keeping your phone standing up so you can see the screen while you're typing. The good news is that there are smartphone stands available starting from $1. You can find them in your favorite electronics store or you can do a Google search under "smartphone stands" (without the quotation marks).

If you're really cash-strapped and/or you're the crafty type, you can make your own. CNET has an article about how you can make your own smartphone stands using common everyday items like a business card along with links to free patterns and tutorials so you can try your hand at making one. (https://www.cnet.com/news/six-free-diy-smartphone-stands/)

As for storing files, you can store them on your smartphone's hard drive as well as store them in the cloud. The disadvantage is using your smartphone's hard drive is that, after a while, your disk can get full, which will affect the reliability of your smartphone. You'll need to get at least one cloud storage account as a place where you can put your files.

There are a lot of cloud storage companies out there but I'm going to focus on just two of them because they are not only among the most well known of the cloud storage services but they are also affordable options for the cash-strapped person: Dropbox and Google Drive. Both are pretty easy to use. You can not only store your files in the cloud while not having them take up valuable hard disk space on your smartphone but you can also authorize to share your files with others online, which is fantastic if you're collaborating on a project with two or more people. Both have smartphone apps (available for free in the App Store and Google Play) you can use to upload files and you can also access them from a regular desktop computer. What's more, both have an "Undelete" option in case you accidentally deleted a file that you didn't mean to delete. (The only caveat is that a recently deleted file will only remain on the server for a certain amount of time. Once that time has passed, the file will be permanently deleted and you will never get it back again.)

Dropbox offers a free basic account that includes 2GB of free space. If you need more space, Dropbox offers a Plus plan that includes 1TB of storage for $9.99 per month and a Professional plan that includes even more features than the Plus plan. https://www.dropbox.com/

Google Drive, which you can get for free when you sign up for a Google account, provides 15GB of free space which, on the surface, sounds even more generous than what Dropbox offers for free. But there's a catch: The limit not only includes what you put on your Google Drive but also what you have in your Gmail account (including messages and attachments), and Google Photos. While CNET has a helpful article on how to declutter your Google Drive without making major deletions of your important files (https://www.cnet.com/how-to/how-to-free-up-google-drive-space/), you'll still need to keep tabs on your Google Drive in order not to go over your free space limit. If you need more storage, Google Drive offers paid options ranging from $1.99 per month (for 100GB) to $99.99 per month (for 1TB with each additional TB costing an additional $99.99 per month). https://drive.google.com/

I personally have accounts with both Dropbox and Google Drive mainly because I do work for different people who prefer either one or the other and I need the flexibility based on the client's personal preference.

Obtaining a Computer on a Very Limited Budget: Buy Used

While using a smartphone is a low-cost computer alternative, there comes a time when you're sick of dealing with tiny screens and cloud computing. You just want a regular computer. There are affordable computers that are available for people on a limited budget.

Microsoft Registered Refurbisher Program has a database of computer resellers located both in the U.S. and abroad who are authorized to sell used computers with Microsoft Windows installed on them. If you are a cash-strapped Windows user who wants to stay with that operating system, this is the site for you. https://www.msregrefurb.com/RRPSite/LoginPage.aspx

Mac of All Trades is a reseller of used Apple Macintosh computers and peripherals. http://www.macofalltrades.com/

Macincloud is for those who only need to use an Apple Macintosh for a short period of time but, for whatever reason, it is not feasible to permanently own a Mac. For a rental fee you can use your own computer (regardless of whether it's Windows or Linux) to access Mac apps and files online through the Internet. https://www.macincloud.com/

Do you need to own a Mac computer but can only afford a used PC? **Hackintosh** has free instructions on how you can install the various Mac OS X versions on your PC. https://hackintosh.com

refurb.io sells used Lenovo computers. https://us.refurb.io/

eBay is a good resource for finding used computers at affordable prices. What's great is that if a deal goes bad in any way, you can report that person to eBay. If you used a credit card or PayPal for your purchase, you can also open a dispute with them as well. https://www.ebay.com/

Craigslist can also be a good resource for finding used computers at affordable prices. Craigslist is a bit riskier than eBay since all transactions are typically done in person using cash and, unlike eBay, you can't rate your seller—which is bad in the case where someone sold you a computer that turned out to be a dud or if the person is only pretending to sell a computer and he/she literally takes the money and run without giving you anything. The bottom line is that you can find some good deals and most of the transactions go well without incident. Just take a few precautions and always ask the seller to allow you to try out the computer before you buy it just to make sure that it still works. One helpful hint: Many police stations across the country have allowed their facilities to be used to conduct in-person transactions. They are generally located in the front lobby, open 24 hours a day, and have closed circuit TV cameras pointed at all times. Contact the police in your area to confirm this. https://craigslist.org

Facebook Marketplace is Facebook's attempt at taking on Craigslist for the local sales market of used products. Unlike Craigslist, you must be a registered user of Facebook in order to sell on its marketplace. Like Craigslist, most of the transactions are done in person. Unlike Craigslist, if something goes wrong with your transaction, you can report that person to Facebook. You can minimize the risk of being ripped off by asking the seller to allow you to try out the computer before you buy it just to make sure that it still works.

https://www.facebook.com/marketplace/104251676279233

In addition to Facebook Marketplace, Facebook also has a variety of **online yard sales groups** where you can look for computers as well. These online yard sales groups are categorized by towns, counties, and states. Just do a search on Facebook for "[Name of city/county/state] yard sale" (without the brackets and quotation marks) in order to find the online yard sale groups that are in your area.

Local flea markets. I've also seen used computers and peripherals sold at local flea markets with prices starting at $25. This option can be a godsend for people who are really broke. Keep in mind that not all flea market vendors will accept returns if something goes wrong. Many of these computers and peripherals may not come with users manuals. A good workaround is to do a Google search on "[COMPUTER MAKE AND MODEL] manuals" (without the quotation marks and brackets) because you can frequently find free manuals in a .pdf format that you can download. I've used this option many times myself when I couldn't locate a manual to something I needed to use. Many of these flea markets are operated every weekend. To find one just do a search on Google under "flea markets near me" (without the quotation marks).

Give new life to an outdated computer. Here's the situation. You have an old PC with a very outdated version of Microsoft Windows but you can't update it to the latest Windows version because the hardware is also very outdated. Before you toss it into a landfill, you can convert it into a Linux computer.

Linux takes up less hard disk space and RAM than Windows so it's an ideal operating system for older computers and you can get more years of use out of that old PC. Here is how you can do this.

First, back up any important files you have on to USB flash drives or external hard disks because there's a strong chance that installing Linux will erase whatever you have on your computer hard drive. Next is to get a hold of a USB flash drive that has Linux installed on it. You can buy them at places like Bonanza (https://www.bonanza.com/), OSDisc (https://www.osdisc.com/), or Amazon (https://www.amazon.com/).

Once your USB flash drive arrives, install Linux on your computer. If you need help in this, you can check out these free tutorials on ZDNet (https://www.zdnet.com/article/how-to-install-linux-mint-on-your-windows-pc/) or Instructables (https://www.instructables.com/id/Install-any-linux-from-a-usb-the-easy-way/).

Next you'll need to learn how to use Linux. There are free tutorials out there where you can master Linux in no time at all at the following sites:

https://www.lifewire.com/beginners-guide-to-linux-4090233

https://www.wikihow.com/Use-Linux

https://www.pcworld.com/article/2918397/operating-systems/how-to-get-started-with-linux-a-beginners-guide.html

https://lifehacker.com/how-to-get-started-with-the-linux-operating-system-1819644874

https://maker.pro/linux/tutorial/basic-linux-commands-for-beginners

Once you install Linux, you'll need new Linux-dedicated applications. Later in the book I have a list of open source alternatives to major software packages from companies like Adobe and Microsoft that you can download for free for Linux. All of these packages will export your files into the popular file formats (such as .doc, .jpeg, .gif, .pdf, etc.).

Obtaining a Computer on a Very Limited Budget: Buy a Cheap New Computer

If you're a cash-strapped person who prefers a new computer, Linux is the best way to go. Not only do Linux computers tend to be cheaper but you can download a bunch of open source software (including video editing, word processing, and more) for free. You can also find free Linux tutorials on the Internet (especially on YouTube) if you have never used that operating system before.

The only confusing thing is that Linux, which is an off-shoot of Unix, comes under many different variations, such as Linux Mint, Ubuntu, Raspbian, Chrome OS, and Debian. They all work the same and uses most of the same apps (with the exception of Raspian, which is made especially for Raspberry Pi, and that's because that particular computer has less memory and hard disk space).

Here are just a few of the more affordable Linux computers you can purchase.

Raspberry Pi starts at $5 (for the Raspberry Pi Zero) but you only get a computer board with no peripherals (including a case). I generally recommend buying a kit (especially if you're a computer newbie) from websites like Allied (https://www.alliedelec.com/), Adafruit (https://www.adafruit.com), Micro Center (http://www.microcenter.com/), Newark Element 14 (http://www.newark.com/), Pi Shop (https://www.pishop.us/), Cana Kit (https://www.canakit.com/), or Chicago Electronic Distributors (https://chicagodist.com/) because, for just a few more dollars, you'll not only get the Raspberry Pi board but also a case to protect your board, a mouse, a keyboard, and an SD card with the operating system. (Usually it comes with Raspbian, which is a version of Linux that's designed specifically to work with the Raspberry Pi. But there are other operating systems—including one that's based on Microsoft Windows—that one can use instead. For more details, see https://www.zdnet.com/pictures/top-raspberry-pi-operating-systems/) On top of it, there are plenty of apps that you can download for free, such as word processing (https://www.makeuseof.com/tag/use-your-raspberry-pi-like-a-desktop-pc/) and games (https://eltechs.com/gaming-on-raspberry-pi/).

Chromebooks start at $85 and they range from little sticks where you plug into your television's HDMI port while you have to come up with a mouse and keyboard (both of which can be found cheaply if you shop around) to regular laptops. https://www.google.com/chromebook/find-yours/

The Pine 64 computer starts at $100. https://www.pine64.org/

Lenovo computers start at $160 (for the Lenovo ThinkPad N22) and it comes with your choice of Windows or Linux. https://www.lenovo.com/

Acer computers start at $300 (for the Acer Spin 1 SP111-31-C2W3) and it comes with your choice of Windows or Linux. https://www.acer.com/

System76 Lemur starts at $699 but they do offer personal financing plans for the cash-strapped. https://system76.com/

How to Print Documents If You Don't Own a Printer

If you need to print something but, for whatever reason, you don't have a printer, there are a few alternatives you can pursue. One is to download your documents on your USB flash drive and take them to your workplace. Upload them on your work computer then print them out.

If your company prohibits using its equipment for personal use or if you're using a smartphone as a computer, then you can have your documents printed out using one of the following stores:

FedEx Office will print your documents if you attach them to an email. Send the email to printandgo@fedex.com then wait for a confirmation email (which generally takes no longer than a few minutes). Then go to your nearest FedEx Office store and go to one of the self-serve machines. Check and make sure you have enough money on your self-service card. Using the touch screen, select "Print" then "Print with Retrieval Code." Enter the retrieval code that was sent to you in the confirmation email then print your file. To find the nearest FedEx Office store: https://www.fedex.com/en-us/office.html

Staples offers a similar service. Attach your file to an email then send it to staples@printme.com. Wait for a confirmation email (which generally takes no longer than a few minutes). Then go to your nearest Staples store and go to one of the self-serve machines. Check and make sure you have enough money on your self-service card. Using the touch screen, select "Print" then "Email." Enter the eight-digit confirmation code that was sent to you in the confirmation email then print your file. To find the nearest Staples store: https://www.staples.com/

You can also go to **your local public library** where you can print your documents in exchange for paying a small fee. All you have to do is put your documents on a USB flash drive, borrow one of the library computers, then send them to the printer. If you need help in doing this, ask a librarian.

How to Scan Documents if You Don't Own a Scanner

The camera feature of your smartphone generally makes a good alternative to a scanner. But in those instances where you need to produce a high resolution document, here's an app that will help you out without needing to buy a scanner.

PhotoScan is a free smartphone app where it functions like a scanner. All you have to do is to place the document on a flat surface, then start PhotoScan. The app will take one initial picture then will tell you which points to focus your smartphone and take individual pictures of those areas. Then it compiles all of those pictures into one high resolution document. PhotoScan is available in the App Store and Google Play.

If you're in a really tight pinch, you can use scanning services that are offered by **FedEx Office** and **Staples**. For the locations nearest you, check the following websites.

FedEx Office: https://www.fedex.com/en-us/office.html
Staples: https://www.staples.com/

The Internet Zone

A still from an animation I did in the 1990s, which you can view online at https://youtu.be/ScYL89nQAMk

How to Access the Internet on a Very Limited Budget

In the U.S. the major telecom and cable companies have pretty much dominated the Internet access market thanks to numerous mergers and acquisitions that had been going on since the 1990s. Many of these companies will do a bait and switch where they will give you internet access (which is sometimes bundled with a cellular phone plan) for a low price of anywhere between $75-80 per month for the first year or two then they will abruptly raise their rates to something like $150 per month or higher. They will also try to pressure you into purchasing an Internet/cellular phone bundle with cable television (after all, many of these companies started out as cable TV companies) for an initial low monthly price until they start to gradually raise their rates on you.

What's more, if something goes wrong with your Internet access, many of these companies tend to be very slow at resolving the issue mainly because they are monopolies in many parts fo the country so, with no competition, they don't have to respond quickly because their customers frequently have no other options and the companies know it.

But there are some earnest attempts by smaller companies to provide Internet access and try to break the monopolies that have gotten their grip on the U.S.

NetZero was a pioneer of free Internet access in the late 1990s and it's still going strong by offering low cost Internet services. It offers free wireless plans for less than 200MB (which is good for reading emails and text-based sites) but their paid wireless plans start at $17.95 per month for 500MB of data. You can either buy a NetZero hotspot for $79.95 or you can bring your own hotspot device to this service.

https://www.netzero.net/

Karma has two plans. One is Drift, which is meant for people who only need to access the Internet when they are on the road and they don't want to pay the high hotel prices for using its wi-fi. You pay $3 per month and $10 per GB. The other plan, Pulse, is a monthly plan with subscription prices starting at $39.99 per month for 5 GB. With both plans you need to purchase one of two available portable wi-fi devices. There's the white and orange device that costs $199. But if you prefer to anonymously surfing the Internet, Karma has a black device that will hide your location and identity with prices starting at $308.98. Karma has a referral program where you can earn credits on your plan if you refer a friend or relative to Karma. https://yourkarma.com/

FreedomPop has a plan where you pay nothing per month if you use less than 500 MB each month, which is perfect if you only access the Internet to read emails and text-based documents. If you use more data, it has prices starting at $19.99 for 2 GB. You get a Netgear Unite Internet Hotspot for free and you pay a one-time activation fee of $9.99. https://www.freedompop.com/

If you can't afford to even pay for these alternate Internet plans there are a few places you can go where you can access the Internet for free with no purchase required.

The vast majority of **public libraries** offer free wi-fi. Some libraries require that you sign up for a free library card before you can use its wi-fi while others don't have that requirement.

Many **shopping malls** offer free wi-fi as well. All you have to do is bring a smartphone or laptop, sit on a bench in the middle of the mall and start surfing away. Sometimes the mall may ask you for an email address as a condition of using its wi-fi but it's no big deal. (If you're leery about giving away your personal email address, you can always get a free Gmail or Hotmail account that you only use in situations like this.) In case you're wondering, I've never had a mall security guard try to hassle me or encourage me to move or anything like that. That's because the security guards are more focused on shoplifters or obnoxiously loud troublemakers than a person who is quietly sitting down and surfing the Internet.

Barnes & Noble offers free wi-fi and you don't have to purchase anything to use it. Most of these stores have a Starbucks cafe inside so you can sit down, get comfortable, and surf away. You can find the nearest store at the bottom right-hand corner of this page at https://www.barnesandnoble.com/h/cafe

Certain **McDonald's** locations offer free wi-fi. You can purchase a soda (and maybe even some food from their dollar menu), find a table, and surf away. You can find which McDonald's has the free wi-fi in your area at https://www.mcdonalds.com/us/en-us/restaurant-locator.html

Starbucks offers free wi-fi at all of its locations. https://www.starbucks.com

Panera Bread also offers free wi-fi at all of its locations. https://www.panerabread.com/

Buffalo Wild Wings in another place that offers free wi-fi. https://www.buffalowildwings.com/

Whole Foods Market gets frequently derided as "Whole Paycheck" because of the prices of its organic food but it does has free wi-fi plus there's a cafe where you can sit down and surf away online. https://www.wholefoodsmarket.com

Wegmans is a grocery store chain that offers free wi-fi. It has a Marketplace Café where you can sit down and surf online. https://www.wegmans.com

Target offers free wi-fi at locations with a Starbucks cafe located inside of it. https://www.target.com

Dunkin' Donuts is another place that offers free wi-fi at some of its locations. You can find out which ones by going to https://www.dunkindonuts.com/en then clicking on the "Locations" tab.

How to Access the Internet Using Your Smartphone as a Hotspot for Your Computer

Many broke people will use their cellphones as an Internet hotspot. This is accomplished by taking a smartphone, go into the Apps section and select the Settings app. Select "Connections" then choose "Mobile hotspot and tethering." Turn "Mobile hotspot" to "On." Touch the words "Mobile hotspot" and you'll get the name of your hotspot along with the password. Now you can take a computer, a different smartphone, or some other mobile device and turn the wi-fi on. Select the name of your hotspot, enter the password, and you're good to go. Just keep an eye out on the data you use. Depending on the phone company and data plan, you may have to pay extra for any overages.

Many of the major telecoms have dominated the smartphone market. However there are some independently owned companies that are trying to focus on better service along with providing lower rates than the major telecoms. Listed are just a few of these alternate companies. Just shop around online for the best deals and the plans that will fit you the best.

Consumer Cellular https://www.consumercellular.com

Credo Mobile http://www.credomobile.com

Cricket Wireless https://www.cricketwireless.com

Boost Mobile https://www.boostmobile.com/

Net10 Wireless https://www.net10wireless.com/

Build Your Own Internet Access That Benefits Your Community

The previous advice in this section are things that you can do on your own. But imagine what could be done if you and a few other like-minded people in your community would get together and create your own Internet access that would serve as a low-cost alternative to what the major telecom companies are currently offering. This access would offer lightning fast Internet speeds while each user spends little or no monthly cost in order to access it.

It may sound like a hippie pipe dream that should stay in the 1960s but there are some communities that are creating this alternative Internet access that is serving impoverished communities that the telecoms have ignored in places like Detroit and Baltimore.

Building your own community-based Internet access requires a lot of technical knowledge and know-how but here are a few links that can help get you started.

Why Low-Income Communities Are Building Their Own Internet Networks
https://www.fastcompany.com/40540511/why-low-income-communities-are-building-their-own-internet-networks

12 communities experimenting with mesh networks
https://technical.ly/2015/04/06/12-communities-experimenting-mesh-networks/

How to start a community network
https://nycmesh.net/blog/how/

The National Digital Inclusion Alliance
https://www.digitalinclusion.org

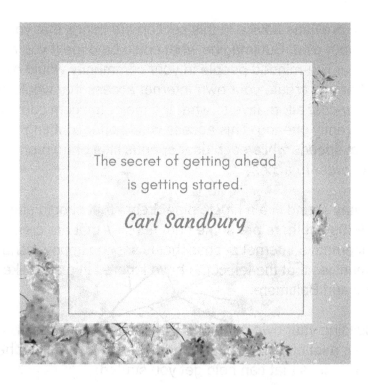

The secret of getting ahead
is getting started.

Carl Sandburg

Free Alternatives to Software Produced By Big Corporations

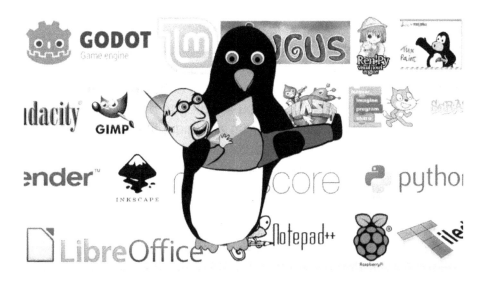

A still from the animation I did for the music video "Open Source is Yours and Mine" performed by Phil Shapiro. You can view it at: https://youtu.be/hEHfhczRWiA

All of the software mentioned in this section are free and legal to download. In addition, many of the developers of the free software have even ensured that their product is virus-free (which is a frequent problem with illegal pirated copies of popular software like Adobe Photoshop).

There is one caveat regarding Macintosh users. Sometimes the Mac OS X will refuse to open a piece of newly downloaded software, especially if it doesn't recognize the server that it was downloaded from. It will give you a dialogue box saying that it can't be opened because it's from an unidentified developer. This feature was originally included in the operating system as a way of preventing viruses from spreading. The downside is that it's too effective, especially if you're downloading from a legitimate site that's virus-free. There is a workaround to this restriction. What you need to do is hold down the "Control" key then click on the application icon once. You'll get a popup menu. Select "Open." You'll get a dialogue box warning that it was downloaded from an unidentified developer and you could be putting the computer at risk for viruses. Select "Open" and your application will open.

Free Alternatives to Microsoft Office

Microsoft Office has long been the industry standard when it comes to office productivity software. In recent years Microsoft has been urging its users to pay a subscription fee for its online Office 365 software but it still does offer standalone versions of its original Microsoft Office for those who don't want to pay a monthly subscription. While Microsoft has recently announced Microsoft Office 2019 for those anti-subscription holdouts (https://www.pcworld.com/article/3228116/software-productivity/microsoft-announces-office-2019-for-customers-who-dont-want-to-pay-forever-for-office-365.html), it's uncertain how much longer Microsoft will continue to make standalone software for computers. The good news is that, for cash-strapped folks, there are alternates to Microsoft Office that you can not only get for free but they can even save files in Microsoft compatible formats (which is useful if you're dealing with someone who insists on Microsoft files). They are all available for Windows, Linux, and Mac OS X unless otherwise indicated.

Apache OpenOffice is a free open source alternative that includes a word processor with a web authoring component, a spreadsheet, a slideshow presentation program, a drawing program, an equation editor, and a database program. https://openoffice.apache.org/

LibreOffice is another free open source alternative that includes Writer (word processor), Calc (spreadsheet), Impress (slideshow presentation), Draw (a drawing program), Base (database), Math (formula editor), and Charts (which creates all kinds of charts, such as a pie chart). https://www.libreoffice.org/

Google offers online apps that you can use for free using just your web browser. If you use a smartphone, you can download the free app versions (which is very handy if, for whatever reason, you need to work offline). What's more, you can collaborate with others online on the same document that you're working on. Google Docs (https://docs.google.com/) is a word processor. Google Sheets (https://docs.google.com/spreadsheets/) is a spreadsheet program. Google Slides (https://www.google.com/slides/) is the presentation software.

Apple iWork is included for free with every Apple Macintosh computer and is considered to be part of the OS X operating system. This package includes Pages (word processor), Numbers (spreadsheet), and Keynote (slideshow presentation).

Free and Not-So-Free Alternatives to Microsoft Windows

Microsoft Windows remains the most popular operating system, despite its numerous flaws over the years (such as being vulnerable to computer viruses, taking up a huge amount of hard disk space, and frequent bugs). There are basically two alternatives to Microsoft Windows. One is paid and the other is free open source. The paid alternative is using Apple Macintosh, which has its Mac OS X operating system. Purchasing a new Mac can be expensive to a cash-strapped person but there are a few lower-cost alternatives that will still allow you to use OS X.

Macincloud is for those who need to use an Apple Macintosh but, for whatever reason, it is not feasible to permanently own a Mac. For a rental fee you can use your own computer (regardless of whether it's Windows or Linux) to access Mac apps and files online through the Internet. https://www.macincloud.com/

If you need to use an actual Mac computer instead of paying a monthly rental fee to access OS X through the cloud, **Mac of All Trades** sells used Apple Macintosh computers and peripherals for prices far lower than buying new. http://www.macofalltrades.com/

If you need to use OS X but you can't even afford to purchase a used Mac, there's a website known as **Hackintosh**, which provides free instructions on you can install

the various Mac OS X versions on your PC.
https://hackintosh.com

The free open source alternative to Microsoft Windows is to use any of the variations of Linux. Here are just a few of the more popular Linux variations, all of which you can download and install on your computer for free.

Linux Mint: https://linuxmint.com/
Ubuntu: https://www.ubuntu.com/
Debian: https://www.debian.org
Elementary OS: https://elementary.io
openSUSE: https://www.opensuse.org
Fedora: https://getfedora.org
Arch Linux: https://www.archlinux.org
Manjaro: https://manjaro.org

Whether you choose Mac or any of the Linux variations, you can still get applications that can do word processing, spreadsheet, animation, music creation, and more. However, there may be times when you need to use a certain application that is available for Windows only. There is are two free related apps for Mac and Linux called **Wine** and **WineBottler** that will open the Windows application in your operating system. Once you download and install Wine and WineBottler, you can download the Windows app of your choice. Every time you need to open the Windows app you have to either right click on the mouse (or, if you have a MacBook, press the "Control" key as you click on the app icon) in order to get a pop-up menu that says "Open With…" Select "Wine" and you're good to go. You can download Wine only at https://www.winehq.org or both Wine and WineBottler at https://winebottler.kronenberg.org/

Free Alternatives to Adobe Creative Cloud

Adobe software has never been cheap but at least you owned the software once you purchased it and installed it on your computer. All that changed a few years ago when Adobe decided to switch to a subscription service where you can only access the applications online and you're expected to pay a monthly fee if you want to continue using Adobe Photoshop, Adobe Illustrator, and other popular Adobe software. Paying a monthly fee (which starts at $50 but how much you pay depends on how many software packages you need to subscribe to) can be daunting to a cash-strapped person. The good news is that there are free alternatives to the Adobe Creative Suite that do not require paying a monthly subscription and they also produce graphics in the popular formats (such as .jpeg, .gif, and .png). They are all available for Windows, Linux, and Mac OS X unless otherwise indicated.

Free Alternatives to Adobe Photoshop

GIMP is a free open source photo editor and graphics application that has long been touted as THE Photoshop alternative. Like Photoshop, GIMP has filters, layers, all kinds of photo editing tools, and animation features. It has an interface that's similar to Photoshop's so switching between the two is no problem if you already know Photoshop. https://www.gimp.org

Seashore is a basic free open source image editing program that's made especially for beginners who feel too intimidated by GIMP and some of the other programs on this list. http://seashore.sourceforge.net/The_Seashore_Project/About.html

Autodesk SketchBook is a program that's free to download for individuals. While this program does allow you to import and edit photos, the primary focus is on illustration and it can accept an electronic pen and drawing tablet (such as Wacom). This program also has a flip book animation feature if you're interested in doing simple and quick animations. There is a SketchBook Pro version that has more features than the free version but the free version has a lot of features that allows any aspiring computer artist to fully express him/herself. https://sketchbook.com

Krita is a free open source painting program that also has an animation feature as well. https://krita.org/

Photos is a photo editing application that is included for free with each Apple Macintosh Computer and iPhone and it is considered to be part of the operating system. Photos may not have the fancy filters or painting tools like the other software mentioned here but it has some nice editing features if you want to do something quick like cropping a photo, eliminating red eye or making a photo lighter or darker in color.

Snapseed is an Android app that functions as a professional photo editor. You can get it from Google Play store.

Canva is a free online resource for those who want to create their own graphics but aren't into using the Adobe Creative Suite or GIMP or any other graphic package. All you have to do is pick your desired size, pick a template, choose a font for your text, add any of the graphic elements that Canva has on its site, then download your creation and start using it. Canva provides plenty of hand-holding so you won't get lost while designing your masterpiece. What's more, Canva allows you to collaborate with two or more people online. Note: Some of the available graphic elements are free to use in your design while others cost money (the prices are pretty low and many of them cost around $1 each) so keep an eye out when selecting your elements. https://www.canva.com

Adobe Spark has a free version for the smartphone that lets you create graphics by picking from photos, icons, fonts, themes, and more. It's available in the App Store and Google Play.

Processing is a free open source graphics software program that's designed to encourage coding for visual artists. https://processing.org/

Free Alternatives to Adobe Illustrator

Inkscape is a free open source vector drawing program that is the most popular Illustrator alternative. (https://inkscape.org)

There's a caveat for Apple Macintosh users—even though there is a Mac version of Inkscape, for whatever reason, the programmers have never created a totally Mac-native program. (I had never seen this as an issue with any other open source Mac programs—all of which are Mac native.) If you want to run Inkscape in your Macintosh, you will need to download and install another free open source program called XQuartz (https://www.xquartz.org), go into the Applications folder, then go into the Utilities sub-folder, click on XQuartz, then select "File," then select "Open...", then open the Inkscape application. Another caveat is that every time there's a major upgrade to the Mac OS X, Inkscape won't run under the new operating system, which means you'll have to wait until the programmers get around to tweaking Inkscape so it'll open under the latest Mac OS X.

GravitDesigner is a free vector drawing program where you have the option of either downloading the software to your computer or using it online through your web browser. (https://www.designer.io/)

Vectr is another free vector drawing program where you have the option of either downloading the software to your computer or using it online through your web browser. (https://vectr.com)

Free Alternatives to Adobe Flash and AfterEffects

While the aforementioned GIMP, Krita, and Autodesk SketchBook does have some animation features, these programs are completely devoted to 2D animation. All are free to download for Mac OS X, Windows, and Linux.

OpenToonz is the open source version of the animation software that was used by Studio Ghibli in many of its classic feature-length anime movies, such as Princess Mononoke and Spirited Away. This software has a very steep learning curve but the good news is that there are plenty of free tutorials out there (especially on YouTube) you can use. https://opentoonz.github.io/e/

Pencil is a free open source animation program that's perfect for beginning animators. https://www.pencil2d.org

Synfig Studios is another free open source animation program. https://www.synfig.org

Free Alternatives to Adobe Fuse

If you're ready to dive into 3D graphics, here are some free software you can check out, some of which also have 3D animation features.

Blender is a free open source 3D animation program. https://www.blender.org

SketchUp Free was originally developed by Google but it has since sold it to Trimble. The free version has a variety of features. If you need more tools, you can always purchase the SketchUp Pro version. https://www.sketchup.com/products/sketchup-free

Wings 3D is a free open source 3D modeling program. http://www.wings3d.com

Autodesk Tinkercad is a free 3D design app. https://www.tinkercad.com

Daz Studio is a free 3D modeling program. https://www.daz3d.com

Mandelbulb is a free program that renders 3D fractals. http://www.mandelbulb.com

Free Alternatives to Adobe Connect

Zoom is free software that allows you to host your own webinar, workshop or meeting. Zoom provides a basic plan that's free where you get to run an online webinar, workshop, or meeting for 40 minutes where you can host up to 100 participants. If you need to host a longer webinar/workshop/meeting or need to host more people, you can upgrade to one of its paid plans with prices starting at $14.99 per month. https://www.zoom.us/

Free Alternatives to Adobe InDesign

Many modern word processing programs have desktop publishing-like templates that are so easy to use that most people can get away with not even touching Adobe InDesign. The word processors I mentioned earlier in this book (Apache OpenOffice's word processor, LibreOffice's Writer, Google Docs, and Apple iWork's Pages) all have desktop publishing-like templates that you can use if you need to whip up a quick flyer or newsletter. But there are times when a word processor isn't enough for a major printing project and you really need an actual desktop publishing program. Fortunately there is an alternative to paying a monthly fee to use Adobe InDesign:

Scribus is a free open source desktop publisher that has a drag and drop interface. https://www.scribus.net

Reedsy lets you write, format, and design an entire book through a web browser for free. https://reedsy.com/write-a-book

Free Alternatives to Adobe Dreamweaver

KompoZer is a free open source HTML web editor where you can churn out websites fast with its drag and drop interface. https://sourceforge.net/projects/kompozer/

SeaMonkey is another free open source HTML web editor. https://www.seamonkey-project.org

Free Alternatives to Adobe Fonts

Whether you're the creative type or you only occasionally churn out flyers for an upcoming community event, fonts can be a great way of adding some pizazz to your work. The good news is that you can find some really cool fonts that are completely legal to download for free.

Dafont https://www.dafont.com

FontZone https://fontzone.net

Freeware Fonts https://www.freewarefonts.com

EKNP http://eknp.com

1001 Free Fonts https://www.1001freefonts.com

Google Fonts https://fonts.google.com/

Still from my animation *The March of Liberty*, which was shown at the 2017 Light City in Baltimore. You can view it at https://youtu.be/AwoF6Q_kI5M

Free Elements to Use in Your Websites, Blogs, Desktop Publishing, Multimedia Presentations, and Other Creative Projects

Free Photos and Clip Art

Here's the situation. You're someone who wants to put out a quick flyer for your church's upcoming picnic or an invitation to your child's birthday party and you need photos or illustrations. Or you have a blog or website and you need some graphics to liven up your site. But you're not much of an illustrator and you are simply not into photography. You also don't have money in your budget to purchase photos or illustrations from places like Shutterstock or Getty Images. The good news is that there are sites where you can legally obtain photos or illustrations for your own use.

Free Stock Photos, which has been online since 1999, is the grandaddy of all those free photo sites and it is constantly being updated with new photos. The photos are free for both non-commercial and commercial uses. http://freestockphotos.com

Pexels is another place where you can get free stock photos. https://www.pexels.com

Pixabay has both free stock photos and free clip art. https://pixabay.com

OpenClipArt.org focuses more on illustrations but there are plenty of clip art images covering a variety of subjects and drawing styles that you can download for free for your own projects. https://openclipart.org

Classroom Clip Art focuses on providing free clip art for students and teachers for use in the classroom but there is still a treasure trove of free illustrations to check out. https://classroomclipart.com

These sites only scratch the surface of what's available. If you can't find what you're looking for, Forbes has a list of 33 sites where you can obtain stock photos for free. https://www.forbes.com/sites/tomaslaurinavicius/2016/03/07/free-stock-photos/#51227e063624

Free Apps for Podcasting, Screencasting, Videomaking, and Musicmaking

If you're ready to go the multimedia route, here are some free software that you can use to enhance your audio or video prior to uploading it online. The software listed here is available for Macintosh, Windows, and Linux unless otherwise indicated.

Audacity is the free open source audio tool that makes recording and editing audio a breeze. https://www.audacityteam.org

GarageBand is free with each Macintosh computer and it's considered to be part of the OS X system. GarageBand has a drag and drop interface where you can drop loops, change the speed, and change the pitch until you come up with a song that you like then export it into an audio file.

iMovie is free with each Macintosh computer and it's considered to be part of the OS X system. iMovie is a basic video editing program with a drag and drop interface that makes video editing a breeze.

Windows Movie Maker is free with Microsoft Windows and it's considered to be part of that operating system. Like iMovie, Windows Movie Maker also has a drag and drop interface that makes video editing a breeze.

OpenShot is a free open source video editor. Like iMovie and Windows Movie Maker, OpenShot also has a drag and drop interface that makes video editing a breeze. https://www.openshot.org

ActivePresenter is an eLearning authoring software which allows you to do screencasts. It has a free edition for personal and non-commercial use with enough features to do a simple screencast. If you like the software, you can always upgrade it to either the standard or pro edition. https://atomisystems.com/activepresenter/

MySimpleShow allows you to make simple explainer videos doing basic drag and drop through its website online without having extensive knowledge of animation, video production, or multimedia. The Personal account is free while there are paid options that give you even more features (such as removing the MySimpleShow logo watermark and giving you greater control over the content of your video) with prices starting at $125 per month. To sign up for the Personal account, click on the "Make a video for free" button that's located on the upper right corner of the website. https://www.mysimpleshow.com/

JigSpace is a smartphone app that allows you to make free explainer videos using 3D animation with no animation experience required. It's only available for the iPhone, which you can download from the App Store. You can view the animations done with JigSpace on YouTube. (https://www.youtube.com/channel/UCf2oFbbs1PIAAgcMRcDJupw/videos)

Adobe Spark allows you to make explainer videos for free without needing any kind of designer skills. https://spark.adobe.com/make/explainer-video-maker/

Biteable touts itself as The Ultimate Explainer Video Maker and it provides a basic plan for free where you can publish up to 5 videos per month to Facebook and YouTube and have up to 1 GB of storage. https://biteable.com

Powtoon allows you to make animated explainer videos for free. https://www.powtoon.com/

Animatron Studio allows you to make animated explainer videos for free. There's a Studio Mode (https://www.animatron.com/studio) and a Lite Mode (https://www.animatron.com/studio/lite-mode)

Animaker has a free plan that lets you make a two-minute animation. https://www.animaker.com/

Raw Shorts lets you do whiteboard animation and it has a free plan. https://www.rawshorts.com/

Renderforest is another animation creation site that has a free plan. https://www.renderforest.com/

Make Web Video lets you make videos to promote yourself and your business. It's free for low-resolution videos. You only pay if you want a HD version. https://www.makewebvideo.com/

Videopath has a free account where you can make videos without being a videographer. https://videopath.com

Animiz has free software (for Windows only) that enables you to make animated videos and gifs in minutes. http://www.animiz.com

Zoom is free software that allows you to host your own webinar, workshop or meeting. Zoom provides a basic plan that's free where you get to run an online webinar, workshop, or meeting for 40 minutes where you can host up to 100 participants. If you need to host a longer webinar/workshop/meeting or need to host more people, you can upgrade to one of its paid plans with prices starting at $14.99 per month. https://www.zoom.us/

MuseScore is free open source songwriting software. It provides input via either drag and drop with your mouse or using a MIDI keyboard along with a music notation feature so you can print out your own sheet music. It also has a playback feature where you can hear how your song sounds while you're creating your own song. You can export your finished creation in a variety of audio files for use in your projects. I've used MuseScore a few times when I came across some vintage sheet music in a garage sale and I was curious as to what the songs sounded like. (All I did was to copy the notes into the music notation feature then clicked the playback button.) https://musescore.org/en

Clipisode is a free smartphone app that's described as a "talk show in a box." The concept is this: You download Clipisode on your smartphone then you make a short video asking a question. Then you contact your friends via email or social media getting their feedback. The interesting thing is that your friends don't have to have Clipisode downloaded in order to respond to your question—they just click on the link that is provided in your message in order to answer your question. Then you get to review the responses, decide which ones to keep or delete, then upload your show on to Clipisode's servers as well as uploading your same show on the popular social media sites (like Facebook, Twitter, and Instagram). Clipisode is available in the App Store and Google Play.

Are you making a long video that may take up a lot of hard

disk space but you need to know how much room you'll need before you begin? **The Video File Size Calculator** will help you find the answer. https://toolstud.io/video/filesize.php

Are you making a video or some other type of multimedia presentation where you need an excerpt from a video that has already been uploaded to YouTube, Facebook, Vimeo, or some other social media site? **ClipGrab** is a free app where you can simply specify the URL of the video that you're interested in downloading to your hard drive and ClipGrab will do the rest. https://clipgrab.org/

Free Music and Sound Clips For Your Projects

If you're not much of a songwriter and you're not inclined to play around with the likes of Audacity or GarageBand, there are copyright-free, royalty-free music and sound clips that you can download and use in your projects for free. Make sure you read whatever terms and conditions are on these sites. Some sites will allow you to use their sounds for non-commercial uses only while others require that you provide credit to the site where you got the original sound or music from somewhere in your project.

BBC Sound Effects Library http://bbcsfx.acropolis.org.uk/

Freesound https://freesound.org

YouTube Audio Library
https://www.youtube.com/audiolibrary/

SoundBible http://soundbible.com

Free Music Archive http://freemusicarchive.org

Bensound https://www.bensound.com

The Internet Archive's Free Music Archive
https://archive.org/details/freemusicarchive

Free Survey Tools

Sometimes you may feel the need to conduct surveys in order to find out how others like your website/blog/anything you've uploaded online or you may need to organize a meeting and/or workshop (either online or in real life) and you need to find out what others expect to get from that meeting/workshop or even trying to figure out the days and times that people are free so you can schedule your meeting/workshop. Here are some free survey tools that will help get you going.

Survey Monkey https://www.surveymonkey.com/

Typeform https://www.typeform.com/

Google Forms https://www.google.com/forms/about/

Zoho https://www.zoho.com/survey/

SurveyGizmo https://forms.surveygizmo.com/

SurveyPlanet https://surveyplanet.com/

Free Mailing List Software

While many people prefer to make announcements of such things as upcoming exhibitions, latest blog posts, the release of new products, etc. through social media these days, using email and mailing lists still has its place. Not everyone spends much time on social media, which is when using email comes in handy. There are a few free mailing list sites that will handle the mailing and other related marketing things (such as measuring the click-through rate of a certain email campaign) so you can focus on other things in your life.

MailChimp is the big name in providing free mailing list services. The free plan allows you to have up to 2,000 subscribers for sending a limit of 12,000 emails per month https://mailchimp.com/

TinyLetter is a subsidiary of MailChimp and this one specializes in newsletters. Like its parent company, TinyLetter is free to use. https://www.tinyletter.com

MailerLite also provides free mailing list services. The free plan allows you to have up to 1,000 subscribers for sending unlimited emails per month. https://www.mailerlite.com/

"Perseverance is failing 19 times and succeeding the 20th."

Julie Andrews

Free Computer Compilers and Editors for Aspiring Programmers and Coders

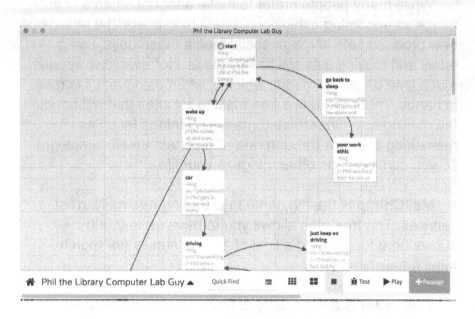

The source code for a game that I did using the open source Twine (http://twinery.org). You can play my game, *A Day in the Life of Phil the Library Computer Lab Guy,* for free at https://sagittariusdolly.neocities.org/games/philthelibrarycomputerlabguy/index.html

There was a time when, if you wanted to try your hand at computer programming on your spare time, you had to pay money to get a Pascal or C++ compiler. These days there are plenty of free compilers and editors where you can try your hand at coding and programming without opening your wallet. If you are unfamiliar with these programming languages, these sites will also provide free tutorials.

Scratch is a free open source coding program that was created especially for children under 12. Adults who are complete newbies at programming and coding may want to give Scratch a try since it covers certain functions that they will encounter with other more advanced programming languages. It has a visual interface and there are lesson plans on the website that you can use to teach yourself. The Scratch program can either be accessed directly online or the software can be downloaded to the computer (which is useful if you don't always have reliable Internet access at home). https://scratch.mit.edu/

Snap! is another programming language that was originally created with children in mind but is touted as being for both children and adults. Like Scratch, Snap! is a free open source coding program that has a visual interface and there are tutorials one the web that one can view for free. https://snap.berkeley.edu

Python is a popular open source programming language that was obviously created by a fan of *Monty Python's Flying Circus* because the compiler used to compile the Python programming language is called IDLE. (As in Eric Idle.) https://www.python.org

Ren'py is an open source game engine that's based on the Python programming language. It emphasizes making interactive visual novels that are similar to those choose-your-own-adventure books that were popular back in the 1980s. https://www.renpy.org

Blockly is an object oriented programming language that was developed by Google. It has an interface that's similar to Scratch and, in fact, Google and the MIT Media Lab's Scratch Team are currently collaborating on the development of a new generation of graphical programming blocks known as Scratch blocks. https://developers.google.com/blockly/

Java is another popular open source programming language. https://www.java.com/

JavaScript is different from Java in that Java is an open source object oriented programming language while JavaScript is an object oriented scripting language. While a Java program can run on its own once it's compiled, something that was programmed in JavaScript can only be run through a web browser. In any case, you can download the free open source JavaScript editor. https://www.javascript.com/

Processing is a free open source graphics software program that's designed to encourage coding for visual artists. https://processing.org/

Twine is an open source language that specializes in creating interactive, nonlinear stories that are similar to those choose-your-own adventure books that were popular back in the 1980s. The finished story is exported in a HTML file where one can run the file using just a web browser. http://twinery.org

Unity is a cross-platform game engine where you can create your own games and interactive multimedia presentations. The Personal version for beginners, students, and hobbyists is free. There are paid versions starting at $25

per month. https://unity3d.com/

MIT App Inventor is a free open source visual programming environment where people of all ages can try their hand at creating an app for smartphones and other mobile devices. http://appinventor.mit.edu/explore/

Scene from an animation I did called *Guitar Love: The Musical*. You can view it online at https://youtu.be/wU4reZBKY48

Creating Blogs and Websites For Free

Sagittarius Dolly
A Blog About My Own Arts and Crafts and Photography

Subscribe to feed   Home   About This Blog (Including Rules and Policies)   Follow Me Everywhere
Contact Me   Past Shows and Awards   Press Clips   Copyright Information

PREVIOUS ENTRIES

Select Month

CATEGORIES

Select Category

NETWORKEDBLOGS

NetworkedBlogs
Blog:
Sagittarius Dolly
Topics:
arts, crafts, opinion

Follow my blog

Check Out My Portfolio Site

August 1, 2018 in Updated Information About This Blog | Comments closed (Edit)

This is my blog about my arts, crafts, and photography along with the occasional rant. If you prefer to view a portfolio of my work, check out this blog's sister site on NeoCities. (Link will open in a new window.) And while you're there, try your hand at playing a video game that I originally designed. 😜

Link-O-Rama

August 18, 2018 in Christmas, Doll Accessories, Doll Furniture, Dolls, Famous People, Free Tutorials, Jewelry, Lessons, Necklaces-Clay, Glass, Yarn, and/or Found Objects, Painting, People | Tags: #MeToo, bot, children, Colin Kaepernick, dollhouse, dreamlike, engagement ring, flower, George Tooker, homeless, husbands, labor rights, Millennium Falcon, Star Wars, stress, surreal, terra-cotta, terracotta, trolls, Twitter, unions, wives, women | Leave a comment (Edit)

Screenshot of my blog, *Sagittarius Dolly*, which you can visit online at https://sagittariusdolly.wordpress.com

Free Blogs

Blogging originally started in the 1990s with the rise of Blogger (which Google later purchased). In recent years blogging have been superseded by the rise of social media sites like Facebook, Twitter, and Instagram to the point where I read the occasional social media post questioning whether blogging is even still relevant today.

I will admit that social media has largely replaced the personal blogs that people used to keep, which documented things like a recent weight loss as the result of adhering to a special diet, the result of the latest round of cancer treatments, their hobbies, the joys and frustrations of job hunting, or their latest once-in-a-lifetime trip to an exotic place. But blogging still has its place on the Internet. Some people may use an anonymous blog to write about something that they would never share on Facebook under their real names because they are afraid that the boss will stumble upon it and they end up losing their jobs. Other people who have a business, who are musicians or who have some other kind of side hustle will use blogging to announce such things as what products they are currently selling or when and where they will be giving their next live guitar performance. Then there are the people who dream about becoming writers so they use a blog to cut their teeth with while hoping that someone discovers their writings and it leads to bigger and better things. Or they might use a blog to make commentaries about the latest news or celebrity gossip in the hopes that they will gain fame a la other bloggers like Ana Marie Cox, Andrew Sullivan, and Perez Hilton.

I have a blog where I write primarily about my arts, crafts, and photography (https://sagittariusdolly.wordpress.com/). I use my blog to go into details about my latest project, such as what materials I used, where I got my inspiration to create this project—in short, I write about the story behind my project, which I can't always do on social media due to character limits (especially on Twitter). While I post my projects on the major social media sites, I still have my blog to write about the things that would be too long for even Facebook.

The topic of blogging would take up a separate book since there are a lot of issues to cover, such as how to write a post that won't result in you getting fired or sued, how to blog without alienating your friends and family, what templates or layouts you should use that won't turn off your potential readers, how to attract readers to your blog, etc. But if you're considering getting your feet wet with a little jump into the blogging pool, here are the most popular blogging platforms for you to consider—all of which offer free accounts.

Blogger is the first major blogging platform that got plenty of attention back in the 1990s. Now owned by Google, Blogger is still going strong. You can get a free Blogger account when you sign up for a Google account. https://www.blogger.com/

WordPress.com is a popular blogging platform that runs off of the free open source WordPress software. There's one caveat: There are two WordPress sites with similar URLs. WordPress.org is meant for you to download the WordPress software on to your computer for free then it's up to you to re-upload it to a server that you have rented from an ISP. If you don't have your own server, then you'll need to use WordPress.com, where you get to post your blog on to WordPress.com's server without needing to download any software then look for your own server space first. WordPress offers a free account with up to 3 GB of storage space for your photos. There are three paid plans where you get more features ranging from $4 per month to $25 per month. https://wordpress.com

LiveJournal is a blogging platform that used to be popular back in the 1990s. It was the first blogging platform I had ever tried. I played around with it for a bit until I deleted it because I was dissatisfied with the direction my blog was going in. (That blog was like training wheels for me where I wrote stuff that I later regretted because I inadvertently hurt someone's feelings and I learned a valuable lesson from that experience.) Unfortunately, I can no longer recommend LiveJournal to anyone—especially to those in the LGBTQ community. That's due to the fact that this platform was sold to a Russian company who then moved all of its servers into Russia and it began to ban certain types of content—especially ones that dealt with LGBTQ issues—in compliance with the homophobic laws that have been passed under Vladimir Putin's regime over the past few years. There have been a mass exodus from that platform as a result.

DreamWidth is a free blogging platform whose code is based on LiveJournal and it seeks to have a similar atmosphere to what LiveJournal was back in the 1990s. The major difference is that it's not subjected to Russian censorship like LiveJournal currently is. https://www.dreamwidth.org

Medium is a free platform that's touted as a community of writers, bloggers, and journalists. It takes more of a magazine approach than a traditional blog in that blog posts are curated by the people who control that platform to determine which posts are worthy of being featured on its main front homepage and on its emailing list that it sends out to those who are registered users. This can provide an opportunity for your writing to be exposed to more people on the Internet but keep in mind that, for every post featured on its homepage and mailing list, there are hundreds of other posts that never get noticed. Its features are minimalist compared to the other blogging platforms but if you're strictly a writer, Medium is worth taking a look at. https://medium.com

Tumblr is a part-social media/part-blogging platform. Like Medium, Tumblr also touts itself as a community but, unlike Medium, Tumblr emphasizes graphics and videos more than the written word. If you're an artist/creative type, you may want to give Tumblr a try. https://www.tumblr.com/

Once you decide on a blog and blogging platform, the biggest challenge is finding new material for your blog. Basically the conventional wisdom holds that if you want to gain a regular following, you generally have to put up a new blog post at least once a week. (The more frequently you post, the more you'll gain followers.) When you first start, you'll have no problem with blogging frequently. However, after the novelty of blogging wears off, it will become more of a challenge to find new material. If you've hit a creative block of some kind, the good news is that there free tools that you can use as inspiration for coming up with the content of your future blog post.

Google Alerts will let you set up certain keywords that are related to the focus of your blog and it will automatically email to you links to articles and other blog posts that you can possibly use as inspiration for new blog posts. https://www.google.com/alerts

AllTop is a site that aggregates articles from media sites all over the world and categorizes them according to topic. If you sign up for a free account, you can create a customized AllTop page that will aggregate those articles which falls under certain topics that you are interested in. https://alltop.com

HubSpot's Blog Idea Generator goes a little bit further than Google Alerts and AllTop. You just type in three keywords that are related to the focus of your blog and this site will churn out a week's worth of blog headlines. All you have to do is write the content that fits those headlines then upload it. https://www.hubspot.com/blog-topic-generator

Article Generator is another free tool where you put in a few keywords and it will generate an article that you can use for your blog. http://articlegenerator.org

The Blog Post Ideas Generator is different from the others in that, instead of entering a keyword or two, you just press an orange button on the page that says "Generate Blog Post Idea" and you get a random topic such as "XX really helps me because…", "Top X_____ Mistakes You Must Avoid", "I couldn't believe it when…", and "Why You Should Always _____ First". The randomness of the suggestions isn't for everyone but if you're so stuck as to what to blog about that you're willing to throw caution to the wind, then you may want to give The Blog Post Ideas Generator a try. https://www.buildyourownblog.net/the-blog-post-ideas-generator/

Free Web Server Spaces

People used to erect their own personal websites in order to express themselves. These days social media have largely replaced many of these personal websites. Despite that fact, I believe that a traditional HTML website still has its place, especially if you're trying to start your own business or if you're showing off your talents because a traditional HTML page will allow you to go further than what social media, with its character limitations and unique layout, will permit. You have a greater chance of directly controlling the look and feel of your own HTML website than a social media page, where you frequently have to strictly conform to that social media platform's layout, character limitations, and standards.

For the cash-strapped person, renting out web hosting space on an ISP's server can be costly. The good news is that there are places that provide free web server space as long as you keep within that web server host's file size limitations. The only downside is that some of these places have content standards as to what you can or can not put on your own website (especially when it comes to images containing nudity and using copyrighted content). But you can't beat having your own website where you don't have to worry about paying a monthly fee. Just make sure that you look up what is the free web hosting service's space limitations along with any policies regarding content before you choose where you will place your new website.

NeoCities is a website that is seeking to revive the spirit of the original 1990s heyday of GeoCities, which was a site that provided free web server space and an online community where fellow webmasters would gather and communicate with each other. (GeoCities was purchased by Yahoo! and it went out of business a few years later.) NeoCities gives you the option of uploading your own HTML files that you created yourself (either through manual coding or using a HTML editor) or you can use one of NeoCities' templates without having to deal with coding. One neat feature of this site is that you can look at other sites that are currently housed on NeoCities' servers and choose which site you want to follow. When you follow that site, you'll receive notifications every time that person updates his/her site. https://neocities.org

Wix lets you create a website without having to do anything even remotely resembling HTML coding. It has a wizard where you can pick templates and decide where to put text and

graphics then it automatically churns out a website for you.
https://www.wix.com

Weebly is another free web hosting site that's similar to Wix in that you can create a website using that web host's wizard without creating a single line of HTML code.
https://www.weebly.com

Jimdo is another free web hosting site where you can build websites without dealing with HTML coding.
https://www.jimdo.com

uCoz is another free web hosting site with templates you can use without dealing with HTML coding.
https://www.ucoz.com/

Webs is another free web hosting site with its own templates so you don't have to deal with HTML coding.
https://www.webs.com

Yola is another free web hosting service with its own templates so you don't have to deal with HTML coding.
https://www.yola.com

Angelfire has been around since the 1990s but not only does it still exists but it also offers a drag-and-drop website builder interface without having to deal with HTML coding.
http://www.angelfire.lycos.com

Tripod is another free web server host that first existed in the 1990s that's not only still around but it offers its own website builder without having to know HTML code.
http://www.tripod.lycos.com

Google Sites, which you get for free when you sign up for a free Google account, not only offers free web server space but it provides templates along with drag and drop so you don't have to know HTML to create your own website. What's more, Google Sites allows you to create as many websites as you want. https://sites.google.com

THE MORE THINGS YOU DO, THE MORE YOU CAN DO.

Lucille Ball

Free For Kids

While there have been debates about how much screen time should be permitted for young growing minds, there's no doubt that, with technology becoming more and more integrated with our daily lives, children will need to learn how to be adept at using technology since their future career prospects will depend on this. There are some free educational software for kids that will not only help them become comfortable with computers and technology but they can practice their typing, math, reading, and art in a fun and entertaining environment. All of the programs below are available for Mac OS X, Windows, and Linux.

Childsplay is a free open source collection of educational activities that's designed to teach your child math, the letters of the alphabet, spelling, and eye-hand coordination. http://childsplay.sourceforge.net/

GCompris is free educational software that's geared for children aged 2 to 10. Activities include reading, arithmetic, science, geography, and more. http://gcompris.net/index-en.html

Stellarium is a free open source program that turns your child's computer into a planetarium. http://stellarium.org

Tux Paint is a free open source art software that's for children between the ages of 3 and 12. Tux Paint is used in many schools around the world and it has a very child-friendly interface that's easy to use. http://www.tuxpaint.org/

Tux of Math Command, from the creator of Tux Paint, is a free open source arcade-style game that's designed to encourage your child to practice math. https://sourceforge.net/projects/tuxmath/

Tux Typing, from the creator of Tux Paint and Tux of Math Command, makes learning to type fun for kids with this free open source application. https://tux-typing.en.softonic.com/mac

Scratch is a free open source coding program for children under 12. Your child can learn how to code computer programs while creating his/her own animation, interactive multimedia, and even games. Once your child is done with a project, he/she can share it by uploading it on to Scratch's servers. The Scratch program can either be accessed directly online or the software can be downloaded to the computer (which is useful if you don't always have reliable Internet access at home). https://scratch.mit.edu/

Snap! is another programming language that was originally created with children in mind but is touted as being for both children and adults. Like Scratch, Snap! is a free open source coding program that has a visual interface and there are tutorials one the web that one can view for free. https://snap.berkeley.edu

Khan Academy provides free lessons for kids in a variety of grades and subject matter. What's more, it offers a free app called Khan Academy Kids for on-the-go learning for your smartphone or tablet. https://www.khanacademy.org

Hour of Code teaches your child how to code using a series of one-hour tutorials, some of which include popular characters like Anna and Elsa from the Disney movie Frozen and Wonder Woman. https://hourofcode.com/us/learn

MIT App Inventor is a free open source visual programming environment where people of all ages can try their hand at creating an app for smartphones and other mobile devices. http://appinventor.mit.edu/explore/

Words Liive has a resource for teachers and anyone who works with children where you can create a culturally responsive lesson plan with just four clicks of your computer mouse or touch screen. You pick a subject matter (such as Albert Einstein), along with modern music that fits with the theme of the lesson plan plus relevant audio and visual elements. Afterwards you can download your lesson plan to present to your students and you can also save your completed lesson plans online for later use. http://www.wordsliivebeta.com/

Kahoot! is a free resource where you and your children can create, share, and play fun learning games. https://kahoot.com

Quizlet is a place where you and your kids can learn with study sets. If they don't see a study set on a topic that they are interested in, they can always create their own. https://quizlet.com

Moodle is an online learning environment for all ages and there are options for kids to create their own lessons. The basic plan is free for up to 50 users with paid plans starting at $57 for up to 500 users. https://moodle.com

It has been a documented fact that there are far fewer women who are working in the computer-related fields than men, which has all kinds of repercussions. (For more on this, I highly recommend Emily Chang's book *Brotopia*, which documents how women have been systematically shut out of Silicon Valley. Cash-strapped people can find this book in a public library or even a used book store.) **Girls Who Code** seeks to combat this trend by organizing girls-only computer clubs where girls can get together, learn how to code, and work collaboratively on various projects. The idea is that, in a supportive environment, girls will feel comfortable enough around computers that they will choose computer-related careers as women. Two Girls Who Code alumni, Andrea Gonzales and Sophie Houser, wrote a book called *Girl Code* about their experiences with this organization, which I highly recommend reading if you want to get the gist of this organization. (You can find this book in a public library or used book store.) You can look at Girls Who Code's website to find a local chapter in your area. If you don't find a local chapter, why not form your own chapter? All you have to do is find other like-minded parents to make this chapter a reality. The Girls Who Code website has everything you'll need on how to form a chapter along with recommended lesson plans and activities so you won't have to wing it. What's more, previous coding experience (or even general computer experience) is not required to form your own chapter—you just need to have the desire to help girls reach their full potential. https://girlswhocode.com/

The UCLA Children's Book Collection has a variety of children's books published between 1863-1999 (including classics like The Wonderful Wizard of Oz, The Adventures of Tom Sawyer, and Mother Goose's Nursery Rhymes) that you can download for free and read with your children. https://archive.org/details/yrlsc_childrens&tab=collection

International Children's Digital Library has free children's books in English as well as a variety of foreign languages, which comes in handy if your child is currently learning a foreign language. http://en.childrenslibrary.org

Wikijunior has free public domain educational children's books in a variety of genres including history, science, geography, and more. https://en.wikibooks.org/wiki/Wikijunior

The Over 50 Zone

A still from an interactive game called *A Day in the Life of Phil the Library Computer Lab Guy*, which I created using the open source Twine software (https://twinery.org/). You can play this game for free at https://sagittariusdolly.neocities.org/games/philthelibrarycomputerlabguy/index.html

Back when the computer revolution first started in the 1990s there were plenty of people over 50 who tended to avoid computers and technology in general and they were able to get by without ever touching anything that even remotely resembled a computer. I know this first-hand because my late mother-in-law was among those who stubbornly refused to use a computer unless she absolutely had no other choice (and it was usually when she was at her job) and she refused to use email. She also used to frequently complain about people who were too reliant on using computers.

But now, thanks to the evolution of laptops, smartphones, and tablets along with faster Internet speeds, it's imperative that an older adult over 50 learn how to use technology and the Internet in order to be able to communicate with their adult children, grandchildren, great-grandchildren, and other relatives—especially if they are of the Millennial Generation or younger.

In order to get an idea of what older adults should learn, check out **10 Pieces of Technology Seniors Should Embrace**. http://seniornet.org/blog/10-pieces-of-technology-seniors-should-embrace/

Libraries, community centers, senior centers, and makerspaces are good resources for finding low-cost or free technical training for the 50+ crowd.

Eldercare Locator will also help you find free or low-cost training courses located in your area. https://eldercare.acl.gov/Public/Index.aspx

AARP once stood for American Association of Retired Persons and it used to be primarily concerned with issues related to retired senior citizens. But this is no longer your parents' AARP. This organization now prefers to be known only by its acronym and it also prefers that people pronounce it as one word (which rhymes with "harp") instead of just spelling it "A-A-R-P." This was done in recognition of the fact that many seniors these days work past age 65. AARP also runs a startup incubator located next door to its headquarters in Washington, DC known as The Hatchery (https://technical.ly/dc/2017/04/06/inside-hatchery-aarp-incubator/). AARP's main website (https://www.aarp.org/) has articles on technology-related issues that could affect seniors, such as being targeted for scam and fraud via a computer or cellphone. AARP also offers Learn@50, which is a variety of free webinars that covers both technical and non-technical topics (such as what to expect from Social Security). https://learn.aarp.org/

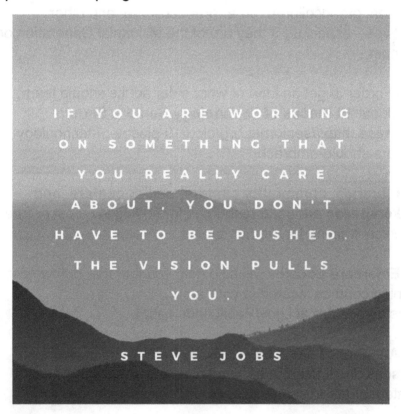

IF YOU ARE WORKING ON SOMETHING THAT YOU REALLY CARE ABOUT, YOU DON'T HAVE TO BE PUSHED. THE VISION PULLS YOU.

STEVE JOBS

How to Obtain Further Education and Training Online Without Losing Your Shirt

A still from an animated music video I did for The Bachelor and the Bad Actress song "Butcher the Hog," which you can see in its entirety at https://youtu.be/llt0Xu25xlw

It's a well-documented fact that tuition at many colleges and universities have risen dramatically since the 1980s and they have even outpaced the rate of inflation. There are plenty of horror stories about students who go to college only to be swamped in high debt after graduation. (https://www.brookings.edu/research/the-looming-student-loan-default-crisis-is-worse-than-we-thought/) In fact there's now a new game show currently in production called *Paid Off* where the winner will have his/her student loans completely forgiven. (https://www.bustle.com/p/how-to-get-on-paid-off-because-the-controversial-game-show-may-be-the-fastest-way-to-wipe-out-your-student-debt-9822153)

Many students had gone into debt attending state-run or private non-profit institutions, which is bad enough. But then there are the private for-profit schools, which have even worse problems. They charge high tuition because they count on students getting financial aid or loans to pay for it. In the case of a student who is also a military vet, these schools are counting on the government funding that vet's education under the G.I. Bill. While there are some for-profit schools that have been in business for many years and have successfully trained and placed generations of people in new jobs (such as Strayer University, which has been in business since 1892), there are many others that have been less successful over the long-run. You can easily check the Wikipedia on failed for-profit schools, such as Computer Learning Centers and ITT Tech, where students paid high tuition fees only to get training using outdated computers and software and they weren't able to find jobs once they completed their studies. (https://en.wikipedia.org/wiki/List_of_for-profit_universities_and_colleges#Closed)

More recently Capella University has been hit with a class action lawsuit by its former students who claimed that the school focused more on its marketing campaign than on providing a top-notch educational program for its students. (https://www.twincities.com/2018/04/23/class-action-lawsuit-alleges-capella-university-lied-about-time-cost-of-advanced-degrees/) Another for-profit school, The Art Institute, has gotten into trouble for offering a sub-standard education that included not hiring enough instructors and using outdated equipment while not providing much outplacement job assistance after graduation. (https://thinkprogress.org/why-students-say-their-degrees-from-the-art-institute-are-worthless-c346be20d899/) As of this writing the new owner of The Art Institute is in the process of closing down many of its campuses nationwide. (https://news.artnet.com/art-world/18-art-institutes-closing-in-us-1318094)

There are also local training companies that provide short-term computer training (many of which last no longer than five days) but the classes can be expensive. With prices ranging from around $500 to $2,500, that option is nearly impossible for someone who is cash-strapped.

You're probably wondering why is getting training from these training companies so expensive. It's because many of these training companies are catering to government agencies and corporations who frequently send their employees to these classes. They can get away with setting high prices because the employers are willing to spend that much without question. I saw this in action myself when I worked in the corporate offices of a now-defunct computer reseller that specialized in selling to the federal government and government contractors. This reseller had set up a training center which offered courses in Microsoft Word, Microsoft Excel, how to use the computer operating system, etc. for its recent customers who wanted to learn how to use what they had just purchased. The company was able to get away with setting a high fee per class (I don't remember exactly how much each class cost but I believe it was somewhere between $300-$500 for a one or two-day class) because the employers were willing to pony up that much money per employee.

Of course if you're out of work and/or in poverty, paying that much money for a class is out of the question. Yet it's a given that, with the frequent changing pace of technology, you'll need to go back for more training but how can one do that without literally losing his/her shirt in the process. The good news is that there are alternatives to having to go heavily into debt in exchange for training.

Free Skills Training Classes

YouTube has all kinds of free training videos in a variety of subjects ranging from coding to auto repair to drawing to cooking. https://www.youtube.com

Codecademy provides free coding lessons in Python, Java, JavaScript, Ruby, HTML, and more. https://www.codecademy.com/

Khan Academy provides free online classes for all ages in a variety of subject matter including math, science, economics, computers, test preparation, and more. https://www.khanacademy.org

Saylor Academy has free online courses where you can actually earn college credit and even earn certificates. https://www.saylor.org/

edX has free college-level courses provided by top-notch universities like Harvard, University of California Berkeley, MIT,

Sorbonne Université, and more! https://www.edx.org

Open2Study is an Australian-based site that also provides free college-level courses. https://www.open2study.com/

Alison provides free training courses where you only pay if you need a certificate for completing a course. https://alison.com/

HubSpot Academy provides free training courses in subjects related to sales and marketing. https://academy.hubspot.com

Coursera lets you learn skills from top universities for free. https://www.coursera.org/

GCF Learn Free is for those who feel that their technical skills aren't up to snuff. It provides free courses in basic computer skills, such as using Gmail, Microsoft Office, Linux, Windows, and Mac OS X. https://edu.gcfglobal.org/en/

AARP offers **Learn@50**, which is a variety of free webinars that covers both technical and non-technical topics (such as what to expect from Social Security) for people over 50. https://learn.aarp.org/

Lynda lets you learn a variety of skills and even earn certificates, which you can then post automatically on your LinkedIn account. (That's because Microsoft owns both Lynda and LinkedIn.) Lynda is strictly a paid subscription service but you can access this for free through many public libraries throughout the country. The only caveat is that, in order to access the free classes, you have to use a link on your public library's homepage instead of going directly to Lynda's website. If you need help in doing this, ask a librarian.

Free Foreign Language Classes

With more and more jobs ads requiring prospective employees who can speak at least one other language besides English (usually Spanish but I've also seen job ads looking for people who can speak Chinese, Korean, Vietnamese, and French), it is now generally a good idea to be familiar with at least one foreign language. The good news is that there are online places where you can master a foreign language anytime at your own pace for free.

Duolingo takes a gaming approach to learning a foreign language where you spend just a few minutes a day on the language of your choice. It has a variety of languages to choose from, including Klingon and High Valyrian (which should be of special interest to fans of *Star Trek* and *Game of Thrones*). This site is perfect for beginners who have never studied a certain foreign language before. This site also has stories, podcasts, and flash cards where you can further practice your chosen language. If learning via computer isn't enough for you, Duolingo also has a list of events in your local area where you can practice your chosen language with other people. https://www.duolingo.com/

Clozemaster is a site where you practice your vocabulary. This one is geared more towards those who have been studying a foreign language for a while. It provides the perfect opportunity to practice your listening skills, especially if you're planning on traveling to a foreign country or if you have to deal with immigrants who haven't mastered English yet. https://www.clozemaster.com/

Open Culture has a list of resources where you can study the foreign language of your choice for free.

http://www.openculture.com/freelanguagelessons

Rosetta Stone has long been praised for its innovative method of teaching foreign languages, even if this program costs money. The good news is that many libraries offer free access to Rosetta Stone if you have a library card. The big caveat is that you can't go to Rosetta Stone's main website in order to access the free lessons. Instead you'll have to go to your library's website and click on the Rosetta Stone link. If you need help, talk to your librarian.

Transparent Language Online is another paid foreign language program that you can access for free through your public library if you have a library card. Like Rosetta Stone, Transparent Language Online has to be accessed through your library's website. If you need help in accessing this, talk to your librarian.

ROBOHEDGY

The Job Zone

Free Online Job Search Resources

If you're cash-strapped, chances are that you'll need to find a job (or two or three) so you can make enough money to support yourself and your family. There are so many different facets of the job hunting experience that one could easily write a separate book on 21st century job search strategies. I'm just going to scratch the surface by listing some free online resources that could help you find your next opportunity.

Meetup is the perfect site for finding networking opportunities in your area. Once you sign up (which is free), all you have to do is search for areas that you are interested in, join groups that are related to your areas of interest, then go out and meet people face-to-face. Keep in mind that while some Meetup groups meet for free in certain public areas (such as in a public park or in a local library), many others will meet in a bar, restaurant, or cafe so you'll need to bring some money with you when you go out. (You can keep costs down by limiting yourself to just one drink and eating a snack or a meal before arriving at your destination so you won't have to spend as much money on food.) Meetup is a great way of meeting someone new and there's always the chance that this new person might have a job lead for you. As the old saying goes, "If you want to get ahead in your career, it's not what you know, it's who you know." https://www.meetup.com/

LinkedIn is the social media site for professionals. While there are opportunities to attend local networking events where you get to meet face-to-face with other people in your area like Meetup, LinkedIn is more focused on initially meeting new people virtually. It's structured similar to Facebook in terms of being able to like posts, upload photos/videos, and making contact with other people who either live in your area or live several time zones away. There are groups you can join that are either related to your current field or the field that you would like to be working in. The big difference is that there's a subtle pressure against sharing cat memes or your photo of what you've just ate for dinner tonight or making overtly political posts. (I've personally seen what happened when people tried attacking the current government or taking a stand on a very controversial political issue on LinkedIn and it's not a pretty sight. If you need to get political, I would strongly advise you to use Facebook or Twitter instead.) Basic membership is free. There are four separate Premium plans where you can get more features (such as unlimited contacting of people whom you're not currently connected with) ranging from $29.99 per month to $119.99 per month (the latter is aimed at recruiters). There are plenty of free tutorials out there on how to job hunt on LinkedIn without signing up for a Premium plan that you can access by doing a simple Google search. There are also books that you can check out of your local public library on how to use LinkedIn effectively. https://www.linkedin.com/

Jobcase is a newer work-related social media site that's similar to LinkedIn, except Jobcase is more focused on non-executive positions like retail clerks, landscapers, administrative assistants, forklift operators, and other jobs that don't require advanced degrees. This site does have community groups that you can join in order to get advice on how to apply for a job with a certain company or get leads on a company that's hiring soon. Jobcase is also entirely free to join with no premium packages or anything like that. https://www.jobcase.com/

If you're 50 and older **AARP** has a job board that you can sign up for, which matches employers with mature workers. https://jobs.aarp.org

JobFlare is a free job hunting smartphone app with a unique premise: Instead of sending a resume and cover letter to a company only to have it completely ignored, you play a video game that gives the hiring company an idea as to how you would perform on the job. JobFlare can be downloaded for free from the App Store or Google Play.

Shapr is a free smartphone app that's been described as "Tinder for professionals." It has a similar interface to Tinder but instead of looking for a date, you are looking for people to meet in person and network with. When you first sign up you mention what you're interested in and Shapr will try to match you with people who share similar interests. Each day you are given a bunch of people's profiles to look through. If you like what you see in a certain person, you swipe right. If that person doesn't interest you in any way, you swipe left. Afterwards you can make arrangements with the other person to meet with you either online or in real life. Shapr can be downloaded for free from the App Store or Google Play.

Free Printables has templates in its Printables for Business section for your favorite word processor or desktop publishing program that you can download for free and use in your job search—including resumes/CVs, cover letters, thank you letters, and business cards.
https://www.freeprintable.net/#business

It can be a challenge to write a cover letter that will encourage prospective employers to view your resume. Here are a few links loaded with free advice on how to write a cover letter that will wow the hiring manager.

How to Write a Cover Letter: 31 Tips You Need to Know
https://www.themuse.com/advice/how-to-write-a-cover-letter-31-tips-you-need-to-know

The Art of the Cover Letter: Tips for getting noticed and getting an interview
https://executivedrafts.com/the-art-of-the-cover-letter-tips-for-getting-noticed-and-getting-an-interview/

MySimpleShow allows you to do animated explainer videos without having any extensive knowledge of video making or animation. Among its available templates is one where you can highlight your work experience and achievements on previous jobs, which you can show to your potential employers in order to impress them under the Personal plan, which is free. All you have to do is select "Make a video for free" button that's located on the upper right corner of the website. https://mysimpleshow.com/

Are you stumped on what career you really want to pursue? Can't decide between two or more potential careers? **O-NET Online** can help. It provides a list of careers along with information on whether a certain career field is growing or not. https://www.onetonline.org/

It's a well-known fact that recruiters and hiring managers these days will scan your resume using software known as Applicant Tracking Systems (ATS) in search of certain keywords. If your resume fails to return enough keywords, it gets rejected. **Jobscan** is a free service where you can scan your resume and the ad featuring the position that you're applying for and it will tell you how much your resume matches that job ad. It gives you a chance to revise your resume so it'll be more likely to pass that ATS and have a human actually read it. The only caveat is that you only get five free scans per month. (There is a paid subscription option where you can make multiple scans in a given month.) If you're applying to a lot of jobs, you can take two or more similarly worded job ads and put both your resume and one of the ads through Jobscan once. https://www.jobscan.co/

TagCrowd has a free service where you can put a job listing into its field and it'll give you the buzzwords or tags for this listing. This can help you customize your resume to fit this job in order to get through the ATS software. https://tagcrowd.com/

Ask the Headhunter is a valuable resource that provides free job hunting tips from an expert who's been providing such advice online since 1995. https://www.asktheheadhunter.com

Your local public library may have free resources where you can use your library card to access such things as free online feedback on your resume or trying to figure out what career opportunities you might want to pursue. These resources vary from library to library so ask your local librarian for more details.

And here are some job hunting resources that the experts frequently cite as the ones you should be using. However, after my less-than-thrilling experiences with these sites that resulted in no job, I can't recommend them at all. They are a colossal waste of time that you need to avoid at all costs.

Indeed.com is the largest job search engine. It aggregates jobs that are supposed to be currently open but, based on my own experience, the jobs listings that frequently come up in searches tend to be out of date. While I have a few friends who had found jobs through Indeed, I never had much luck myself. Of all the jobs I applied for through Indeed's website, I only got one interview—and that one didn't result in a job for me. My advice is that if you use Indeed for your job search, go directly to the website of the company behind a certain job listing (you can do a Google search for the company's URL if necessary) and verify that this company is really hiring. If the company is really looking for employees, submit your resume directly through that company's website or to the email address of the hiring manager. Do not submit your resume to the hiring company through Indeed.com because there's a chance that it will just go down the proverbial black hole and you'll never hear anything from them again. Indeed also allows you to upload your resume so prospective employers can find you. I tried it and that tactic ultimately led to nowhere. For more about why Indeed.com is a colossal waste of time, read "The Bogus-ness of Indeed.com" (https://www.asktheheadhunter.com/7152/the-bogus-ness-of-indeed-com) and the user reviews and ratings on ConsumerAffairs (https://www.consumeraffairs.com/employment/indeed.html),

Nexxt is supposed to provide you with the latest up-to-date job listings. You can even join the mailing list so you can get job listings sent to your emailbox. It sounds great in theory but the reality is that, based on personal experience, the listings they send tend to be outdated. Some places I called told me that the job that was listed in Nexxt's mailing list had already been filled a few weeks earlier. I called one temp agency that, according to Nexxt mailing list, claimed to be looking for office workers only to talk to a person at that agency who seemed to be clueless about that ad and told me that his agency was unaware that Nexxt had been listing that agency as looking for new employees. In reality, his agency wasn't looking for more employees and my name was added to a waiting list because all fo the current temp positions had been filled. Worse, I would get new emails several times a day that were filled with out-of-date listings. It also took me several attempts to unsubscribe before I was able to find the link that actually unsubscribed me. If you're looking for work, avoid this site because it's not very reliable and it tends to spam you.

Nexxt also has a subsidiary called **Smart Match** that is just as reliable in providing the latest job listings as its parent company. (In other words, it's not very reliable.) Like Nexxt, once Smart Match gets your email address, trying to unsubscribe is incredibly difficult and it will continue to spam your emailbox on a daily basis. Avoid both Nexxt and Smart Match like the plague.

The Gig Economy

There was a time when, if you needed money fast but you haven't been able to land a job and working in a fast food place isn't appealing to you, you could turn to a temp agency where you can find work fast. (In addition, there were times when temporary jobs ended up turning into permanent full-time jobs with full benefits and a regular work schedule.)

In recent years a series of online platforms, known as the gig economy, have sprung up and it's possible to find work even faster than with a temp agency. The basic gist is this—if you need a job, you go to a certain smartphone app, scroll through the available jobs, then immediately select a job that you want to work at. Then you do the job and you get your paycheck delivered to you via either PayPal or through direct deposit at your bank.

I attended a few workshops with my state's American Job Center where the people there were touting the gig economy as the perfect place to get work quick. Despite the rosy picture that was portrayed in those workshops, there is one unfortunate thing about the gig economy that has sprung up that doesn't get talked about very much in public: There are scammers who use these platforms to take advantage of people looking for work and the job seeker could be stripped of the little money he/she still has.

I was almost scammed by someone who claimed to offer a job through one of those gig economy sites but insisted on doing the job interview via Google Hangouts (which was a violation of that gig economy's platform's Terms of Service because all communications were required to be done through that platform instead of Google Hangouts). As I went along with that person's demand, I found out that what she was proposing sounded like a variation of the notorious Nigerian Prince email scams of the 1990s (you can Google that one if you don't know what I mean). I immediately ended that Google Hangout interview, blocked the interviewer, and reported her to that gig economy platform, which then banned her. I later wrote a detailed story about that experience for LinkedIn Pulse—complete with screenshots of that Google Hangouts interview—to warn others about the scammers lurking on these gig economy platforms (https://www.linkedin.com/pulse/dangerous-potholes-road-gig-economy-kimberly-keyes/).

Basically you're more likely to encounter a scammer if it involves doing virtual work from home for someone in a different part of the country than if you're actually meeting that person face-to-face. In fact, I encountered two more scammers while I applied to virtual jobs. I quickly ended the job interview in both cases because I was just weary at wasting yet more time with these people, especially after that first scammer encounter on Google Hangouts.

While I'm not saying you should never do virtual work, you should be aware of the fact that behind some of those online profiles are some pretty dishonest people. If a person insists on doing a job interview via Google Hangouts or a similar online chat service and refuses to conduct all correspondences through the gig economy platform, walk away immediately.

Another telltale sign that the person who's offering a job is not legit is to look at his/her email address. Let's take someone who claims to be from the Joe Blow Company who's offering you a job. If the hiring person's email address is something like "hr@joeblow.com" or "sales@joeblow.com" or "marketing@joeblow.com" or any address that has @joeblow.com, then there's a good chance it's a legitimate business that has its own website at www.joeblow.com. But if the hiring company uses an email (such as "joeblowcompany@gmail.com") that's from Gmail, Hotmail, Yahoo mail, or a similar free email account, be suspicious. It is most likely a scam and not a real job offer.

Also beware of anyone who is insisting on sending you a check to purchase computer equipment (even if you already own a computer and other equipment) or wants you to deposit a check for a huge sum of money into your own bank account while you withdraw a fraction of that money to send to that person via Western Union. This provides an opportunity for the scammer to completely drain your bank account. For more on this, I highly recommend that you read "Top 10 Job Scam Warning Signs" (https://www.thebalancecareers.com/top-job-scam-warning-signs-2062181).

Even without scammers lurking around, there have been controversy surrounding some of these gig economy platforms. Just spending an hour or two doing a Google search on Uber and its founder, Travis Kalanick, can be an eye-opener.

Aside from scammers, the gig economy has other downsides as well. The work flow can be erratic compared with a regular job and the pay can be low as well. I encountered one gig economy site where you can do 20-minute surveys but the pay was a low 20 cents per survey (or one penny per minute). If you were to do three surveys in an hour, you would make no more than 60 cents, which you really can't live on in the United

States.

Another downside is that there are some gig economy platforms (such as Thumbtack) that requires you to purchase a certain amount of credits before you can even bid on a job. I haven't been able to figure out what happens if you bid on a job and you don't get it—would you get your credits back or would you have to purchase more credits? Basically some of these platforms are requiring job seekers to pay in order to find work, which is the opposite of a temp agency where it is the hiring person or company who pays and not the job seeker.

Some gig economy platforms, such as Upwork, operate worldwide so you could be competing with someone from a country with a lower standard of living (such as India, China, or Vietnam) who can easily afford to work for far lower wages than you can.

You also won't get benefits usually associated with a regular job (such as health insurance) and there are hidden costs as well. For example, Uber and Lift may pay well but, unlike a traditional taxicab company, you are responsible for insurance, gas, and maintenance costs.

I know I sound like a Negative Nellie about the gig economy. I'm not trying to kill your dream of being an independent worker who can work when you want and how you want. I just wanted to give you a sense of the reality of working for a gig economy platform, especially since this topic has gotten tons of positive hype in the mainstream media that bordered on unrealistic expectations. I also wanted to give you as much awareness of the dark side as possible so you won't end up being a victim of one of those gig economy scammers or quitting your full-time job with the expectation that you can do just as well financially relying on the gig economy only to discover otherwise.

There are a few positives with the gig economy. You can work on your own schedule when you want, which is great for those who already have a job or are caring for young children or an aging relative and they really need a flexible schedule. I've read reports of retired people who use the gig economy to earn some extra cash on top of Social Security or whatever pension or 401K plan they have. The gig economy can be a lifeline if you need to pay off a bill quick and you find a platform that will provide you with enough work or money so you can do that.

The gig economy can also be a way for you to potentially explore a new line of work before you commit to a full-time job while getting paid at the same time. For example, let's say you're thinking about going back to school and becoming a veterinarian but you're not sure if caring for animals is right for you. You can try your hand at being a pet-sitter using apps like Rover, DogVacay, and Wag while deciding on your future career options.

The bottom line is that the gig economy can be a good way of making money fast as long as you watch out for scammers, competition with people from countries with lower standard of living, jobs that pay less than $1 per hour, and sites that require you to pay for credits in order to bid on a job. What's more, there are more gig economy platforms that are springing up at a fast rate. One recent example is a relatively new app called Capango, which claims you can find retail work quickly without a resume or filing out a job application. All you have to do is select which areas you're interested in and make a short video about yourself telling the store why it should hire you.

With the number of new gig economy apps coming out on a frequent basis, it's possible that there will be a crash in that area at some point in the future and some of these platforms will go out of business. In the meantime, here are just a few of the gig economy places you may want to check out. Some of these places only conduct business through a smartphone app while others can be accessed through either a smartphone app or a desktop computer. The smartphone apps can all be downloaded for free through either the App Store or Google Play.

If you have a car and don't mind driving people around to various places, there's **Uber** and **Lyft**.

Do you have a car or van but don't mind making deliveries to people's homes? There's **Postmates**, **Shipt**, and **Amazon Flex**.

Do you have an extra car that you rarely use? List it on **Turo** and let other people pay you to borrow your car. Have an RV that you also don't use as much as you thought you would when you first bought it? List it on **RV Share** and let others rent it.

If you have an extra bedroom in your home, apartment, or condo, you can list it on **Airbnb**.

If you're good at typing and transcribing, there's **Rev**.

If you like doing a variety of tasks ranging from assembling IKEA furniture to filing papers to doing bookkeeping, there's **TaskRabbit** and **Moonlighting**.

If you want to work the occasional retail or restaurant job but can't commit to a regular schedule, there's **Capango** and **Snag**.

Do you like working with dogs? There's **Rover, DogVacay,** and **Wag.**

Do you have a car and like working with children? There's **HopSkipDrive.**

Do you have an extra parking space that you rarely use where you live? You can rent it out with **ParkingPanda.**

Are you good with computers and technology in general? There's **HelloTech.**

Do you like to cook for others? There's **Feastly.**

Have a special skill that you can easily teach others? Consider listing your class on **Udemy.**

Are you an artist and/or crafter? You can sell your arts and crafts on **Etsy, Artfire, Big Cartel,** and **Amazon Handmade.** If you want a more consistent monthly income from your admirers that's similar to what artists living in Italy used to get during the Renaissance, there's **Patreon.**

All of the above gig economy platforms are just the tip of the iceberg with more platforms coming online all the time. If you want to explore this topic more, along with getting a list of even more gig economy platforms than what I've already listed here, I highly recommend Angela Heath's book *Do the Hustle Without the Hassle.* (If you're cash-strapped, you can ask your local library about borrowing it or you can try to find it in a used book store.)

For Entrepreneurs Only

You want a job but, for whatever reason, you haven't successfully found one. You tried the Gig Economy platforms but, for whatever reason, they didn't work out either. Yet you have an idea for a product or service that your gut instinct tells you that it has a lot of potential. You need to find a way to turn this idea into a reality.

The good news is that there are now websites that will try to help you make your dreams come true.

Kickstarter is the oldest of the platforms that help raise investor money so you can turn your idea into a reality. Kickstarter holds your hand every step of the way as you make an introductory video, determine your fundraising goals, and raise the necessary cash through that platform. Kickstarter is an "all-or-nothing" deal where if you fail to meet your fundraising goal, your product won't happen and your investors will get their money returned to them. Kickstarter has been an invaluable tool for filmmakers, product makers, musicians, and other creatives in getting their products made and sent to the market. https://www.kickstarter.com

Indiegogo is similar to Kickstarter with one major difference: Unlike Kickstarter's "all-or-nothing" deal where your project won't go ahead if you don't meet your fundraising goal and your investors' money gets returned immediately, Indiegogo will allow your to keep the money you've raised even if you fail to make your goal. https://www.indiegogo.com

Kiva is a non-profit organization that provides loans to small businesses, with a special emphasis on helping businesses that provides some kind of value to the local community, such as a local hair salon or a family-owned cafe.

https://www.kiva.org/lend/kiva-u-s

The Small Business Administration has all kinds of tips, along with documents, showing how one can set up his/her own business. https://www.sba.gov

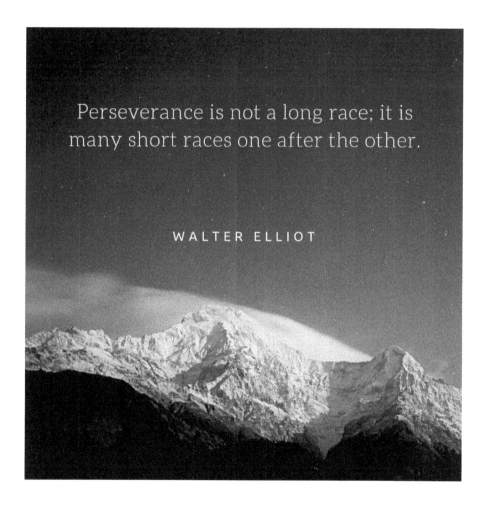

Perseverance is not a long race; it is many short races one after the other.

WALTER ELLIOT

Bitcoin and Other Cryptocurrencies: Don't Believe the Hype

I live outside of Washington, DC, a place where each spring the entire city becomes covered in flowering tulips of all shapes, sizes, and colors. There's even a lesser-known tourist area by the Tidal Basin known as the Tulip Library where you can see the various tulips in full bloom for free if you go there at the right time of the year. Additionally the surrounding suburbs are also frequently covered with blooming tulips in people's yards, outside of office buildings, and local public parks. These days tulip bulbs are relatively cheap to purchase so it makes sense to use some natural beauty as a way of sprucing up the streets, yards, and parks while heralding the coming of spring.

But tulip bulbs weren't always cheap. Way back in the 1600's there was a market bubble in Holland where tulip bulbs became as valuable as gold. It wasn't unusual to purchase a tulip bulb only to have it go up in value just days, weeks, or even months later. There were people who used their life savings to purchase just one tulip bulb in the hopes that it will go up in value and they can resell it for an even higher price. People literally became rich from buying and selling tulip bulbs. This surge in tulip bulb speculation became known as "tulip mania."

Tulip mania abruptly ended in 1637 when the entire tulip bulb market came crashing down. The same tulip bulbs that were as valuable as gold suddenly became worthless in financial value. There were people who literally lost everything all because they poured all of their money into tulip bulbs.

In recent years there have been hype in the media about the rise of cryptocurrencies. The basic gist is this: A cryptocurrency is a money system that, on the surface, is not unlike real-life money systems around the world such as the U.S. dollar, British pound, the European Union euro, Russian ruble, Canadian dollar, Australian dollar, Jamaican dollar, Japanese yen, Mexican peso, etc. Cryptocurrency is a decentralized digital currency that uses encryption to generate money and to verify transactions. Bitcoin is earliest and most well-known of the cryptocurrencies but there are many others.

The big difference is that real-life currencies like the dollar are controlled and regulated by their respective governments while bitcoin and other cryptocurrencies aren't controlled by any government system anywhere in the world. Cryptocurrency uses a distributed ledger technology, such as a blockchain, that serves as a public financial transaction database just like a regular bank. Except a bank usually is regulated by a government while a blockchain or other types of distributed ledger technology has no government oversight whatsoever.

What that means is that if a regulated bank abruptly fails, you can at least recover most of your money. If a blockchain fails, you're pretty much out of luck when it comes to recovering your money.

Most of the major social media sites (such as Facebook, Twitter, and LinkedIn) have banned advertising touting cryptocurrencies. Sometimes you might stumble upon a website or social media post discussing how bitcoin and other cryptocurrencies are wonderful alternative monetary systems that will usher in a new era of a utopia where everyone will live together happily in total harmony and prosperity while earning and spending their bitcoins without worrying about the nasty government intruding in this new blissful utopia. And you can get involved in creating this new blissful bitcoin-powered utopian society by converting some of your hard-earned cash to bitcoin and live happily ever after. Like far out, man, right?

Wrong! The reality is far different and is more likely to result in losing money. Usually in a society, currency is used for two things: 1) as a tool to gain goods and services and 2) as a financial investment tool where the investor hopes to make more money over a long period of time. In the case of the latter, this financial investment tool could be used to invest in stocks on Wall Street or in money market funds or mutual funds. The financial investment tool could also be used in riskier activity in the hopes of getting a big payoff quickly, such as gambling a huge amount of money in a Las Vegas casino or investing in very risky stocks and bonds. The reason why it's risky is because the person could stand to lose a lot of money very quickly if the odds end up not coming in his/her favor.

In the case of cryptocurrency, so far the emphasis seems to be more on making risky investments that may not pay off and cause the person to lose real money in the process. The most notorious of these risky investments was a Japanese bitcoin exchange known as Mt. Gox, whose acronym shows its original origins as a gathering place for fans of the card game *Magic: The Gathering*. (It was originally known as *Magic: The Gathering* Online Exchange.) It soon evolved into a place where people could speculate on bitcoins, which led to bitcoin prices literally shooting up through the roof. Just like the tulip bulbs of centuries ago, some people became rich by speculating on bitcoins. Like all speculation bubbles, this one soon burst, which resulted in people losing their money and Mt. Gox shutting down permanently.

Many experts have compared cryptocurrency to Ponzi schemes and pyramid schemes (see http://thehill.com/opinion/finance/364306-bitcoin-is-a-ponzi-scheme-and-it-will-collapse-like-one and https://www.fool.com/investing/2017/06/14/4-reasons-why-ill-never-invest-in-bitcoin-and-you.aspx). Even billionaire Wall Street investor Warren Buffett has warned people to stay away from cryptocurrency. (https://www.theguardian.com/technology/2018/jan/10/bitcoin-and-cryptocurrencies-will-come-to-a-bad-end-says-warren-buffett) Based on what I've seen so far, I have to agree with them. If you're seriously thinking about investing in cryptocurrency, you might as well just flush your dollar bills down the toilet because that is essentially what you are doing when investing in this virtual money.

Let's take a look at what I wrote earlier about one of the other purposes of currency: a tool that can be used to gain goods and services. So far I have not heard of any mainstream restaurants, businesses, and stores (both in real life and online) deciding to accept any cryptocurrency to conduct business with. The fact that you can't walk into a McDonald's anywhere in the world, order a Big Mac with french fries and a large Coke, and pay for your meal with bitcoin says it all about how useful cryptocurrency really is.

At least tulip bulbs produce beautiful flowers in the spring.

Solid and Inrupt:
Believe the Hype

I'm going to start this chapter with a brief history of the Internet and I'll try to limit the technical geek talk as much as possible. ARPANET was an early ancestor of the Internet that was established by the U.S. Department of Defense in the late 1960s. The Cold War was in full swing and the military commanders were seeking to build a computer communications system without a central core or headquarters because having such a center of operations would leave it vulnerable to a total blackout in the event of a missile strike. With a decentralized system, military people could still continue to communicate with each other even if a nuclear war had started. If one area of communications had been destroyed in a war, the rest of the communications system would still be up and running because of the very nature of having a decentralized system. Access to ARPANET was basically limited to people working in the DOD and researchers at various colleges and universities who were involved in DOD research.

In the 1970s scientists Robert Kahn and Vinton Cerf developed Transmission Control Protocol and Internet Protocol, or TCP/IP, a communications model that set standards for how data could be transmitted between multiple networks. In other words, TCP/IP is the main reason why you are now able to upload a video of your child's piano recital on YouTube or post a selfie photo on Instagram or send an important .pdf document to a colleague via email. ARPANET adopted TCP/IP on January 1, 1983, and from there researchers began to assemble the "network of networks" that became the modern Internet.

Access to the Internet was still limited to people who were geeky enough to manually type cryptic commands at the computer prompt while the average person basically didn't touch the Internet due to the fact that it had an interface that could be hard to learn for a non-technical person.

In 1990 a British scientist working at CERN in Switzerland named Tim Berners-Lee invented the World Wide Web as a way of facilitating communication for scientists in various universities and institutes around the world. To say that the World Wide Web changed life as we know it is an understatement. The World Wide Web made access to the Internet much easier for the less technically-minded person. In 1993 CERN put the World Wide Web in the public domain and the Internet really expanded all over the world to the point where it has gone mainstream.

Tim Berners-Lee never capitalized on his invention for profit, so he never became a mega-rich and powerful computer person on the level of Bill Gates or Mark Zuckerberg. He went on to work at MIT, founded the non-profit World Wide Web Consortium (W3C), wrote a book titled *Weaving the Web*, and he was even knighted by Queen Elizabeth II.

While the World Wide Web flourished there have been some bumps in the road, starting with the great dotcom bubble and subsequent crash that lasted from 1995-2000. (https://en.wikipedia.org/wiki/Dot-com_bubble) In recent years the rise of social media sites like Facebook along with the rise of corporations like Google and Verizon have been trying to vie for dominance on the World Wide Web. Unfortunately this corporate dominance of the web has its downsides, such as leaving corporations vulnerable to having fake news sites originating from Russia flooding the various popular social media sites (like Facebook and Twitter), which had an effect on the 2016 U.S. presidential election. In addition, various companies like Equifax have had its data hacked so your personal data can easily fall into the wrong hands.

Tim Berners-Lee is among those who is trying to reclaim the Internet from being the over-commercialized corporate-heavy online institution it has become and sway it back to his original intention of being a decentralized place where people from all over the world can communicate without having to worry about having their personal data being compromised and harvested by unknown entities or being subjected to fake news from bots.

This reclamation is in the form of two related online entities. One is Solid, which is a decentralized web platform that he and others at MIT have spent years building.

The other is Inrupt, a startup that Berners-Lee has recently launched. Inrupt is going to function the same way that Netscape once did for the World Wide Web (and its successors like Safari, Chrome, Firefox, and Opera continue to do)—provide an easy way to enter Solid.

The best thing about Solid is that one can directly control his/her own data and other people's access to that data. After the numerous breaches of various websites over the past few years, having this kind of control would be welcomed indeed.

Right now both Inrupt and Solid are in their infancy but given Tim Berners-Lee's past record, they have the potential to become the next big thing that's definitely worth learning about now. You may want to start doing Google searches under "free Inrupt tutorials" or "free Solid tutorials" (without the quotation marks) for any free online resources where you can educate yourself about this. In the meantime, you can check out these following links:

"Exclusive: Tim Berners-Lee tells us his radical new plan to upend the World Wide Web," Fast Company, September 29,

2018. https://amp.fastcompany.com/90243936/exclusive-tim-berners-lee-tells-us-his-radical-new-plan-to-upend-the-world-wide-web#amp_tf=From%20%251%24s

Solid https://solid.inrupt.com

Inrupt https://www.inrupt.com

A still from an animation I did in the 1990's, which you can view online at: https://youtu.be/1PdP8uFdFZ0

Accessing the Digital Leisure Lifestyle For Free

There are more to computers than just doing coding or enhancing worker productivity on the job. The computer has become such a necessary tool in our modern society that not having access to a computer can be just as crippling as being illiterate. Even having access to entertainment depends on whether you have access to a computer or smartphone or not. The good news is that when it comes to the digital leisure lifestyle, there are plenty of free options to choose from.

Social Media

Granted social media have gotten its share of flak in recent years as being the perfect places where cyberbullying occurs and fake bot accounts wreck havoc. But it has also become more of a place where people gather online in recent years and it can be a great place to meet new friends and reconnect with old friends from your past. Each social media site listed here could warrant its own book covering topics like how to use a particular platform, how to search for people to connect with, using hashtags, etc. This section just scratches the surface of what's out there.

Facebook is currently the biggest social media site despite the controversy it has undergone in recent years (such as allegations that Russia had setup a variety of fake Facebook pages and accounts in an effort to affect the outcome of the 2016 elections). It was through this site that I've not only connected to people who are currently in my real-life social circle but also people whom I only know through a political discussion .PHP board that I belong to and old friends from college and high school. Plus there are opportunities to make new friends through joining groups that cover a variety of interests ranging from political activism to gardening. Facebook is also taking on YouTube, Craigslist, and LinkedIn by

branching out into videos, an online marketplace, and an online jobs listing. Despite Facebook's recent problems, this site is not going to lose popularity anytime soon.
https://www.facebook.com/

Twitter is another social media site that has also gotten its share of controversy due mainly to President Donald Trump's frequently outrageous tweets. Compared to other social media sites, Twitter is limited to just 280 characters per tweet. It's still a change from the old days when Twitter used to limit its tweets to 140 characters. Recently Twitter has allowed the creation of threads where you upload two or more tweets in a row, which is handy if you have a thought that you really can't limit to just 280 characters. You can also upload up to four photos per tweet and/or one video running no longer than two minutes per tweet. Twitter is more focused on making announcements instead of striking up online conversations with your friends like on Facebook. Compared to Facebook, it can be more of a challenge to follow Twitter conversations between two or more people. Twitter still has its adherents and learning how to make a succinct tweet that includes a hashtag is a pretty useful skill to have in this day and age. https://twitter.com

Instagram (which is owned by Facebook) emphasizes a visual approach where you gain followers based on photos, short videos (one minute or less) and other images you post online. While you can write a caption, it's the image that takes center stage. It has been criticized for its users posting too many selfies but there is plenty of interesting content you can find that don't involve selfies. Like Twitter, Instagram also uses hashtags in the captions, which is the perfect way to get others to discover your pictures. Thanks to hashtags, I've had people liked my Instagram photos several months after I've posted them online. If you're an artist or photographer, this is the social media site for you. https://www.instagram.com

Pinterest is a social media site with interesting twist. When the World Wide Web first came out, your could use a browser to bookmark your favorite sites that you wanted to visit again instead of manually typing the same URL in your browser over and over again. Pinterest is similar to your browser's bookmark feature except that you save a site through "pinning" online to a "board" that you create. You can create boards according to topic or subject matter then pin a site to the appropriate board or boards of your choice. Unlike using your personal browser, your pins can be viewed by other Pinterest users. In addition, someone can follow one of your boards and he/she will be notified every time you make a new pin to that board. In addition, you can follow other people's boards as well. What's more, if you see a pin on someone else's board that you really like, you can pin that particular pin to your own board. This site has especially gained popularity among those who have pinned their favorite recipes, gardening tips, and various craft patterns. https://www.pinterest.com

Membership in **Google+** is included when you sign up for a free Google account. Despite that fact, it is among the less popular social media sites compared to the others and I've heard the occasional online chatter that it may eventually go away one day. Google+ has a similar interface to Facebook and there are self-proclaimed "Facebook refugees" who have made their home on Google+ because they have become alienated by some of the more controversial aspects of Facebook. There are social media marketers who use Google+ extensively because it helps with their SEO results (or search engine optimization results, which is a topic that whole books have been written about). Despite its lack of popularity, you might want to give Google+ a try so see if a smaller, more intimate social media place is right for you. https://plus.google.com/

LinkedIn is a social media site for professionals. It has a similar interface to Facebook, except posting hilarious memes and political opinions are frowned upon there. While it can be used as a tool to land your next job, it can also be used to do some online networking with other people in your field by joining one or more of the many groups on that platform even if you aren't currently in the job market. The basic plan is free and it gives you a lot of access to potential contacts and various groups. There are also a few paid monthly plans if you need a bit more features but most people can get away with just the basic plan. https://www.linkedin.com/

Jobcase is also a professional social media site but its emphasis is on non-executive positions like retail clerks, landscapers, administrative assistants, etc. Unlike LinkedIn, Jobcase provides access to its entire site and features for free. While Jobcase can be used as a tool to land your next job, it can also be used to do some online networking with other people in your field even if you aren't currently in the job market. https://www.jobcase.com/

Minds touts itself as an open source alternative to Facebook that is censorship-free and open to as many different ideas as possible. The platform itself is a mix of left wing/libertarian/alt-right/anarchist politics where it is not uncommon for members to espouse dubious conspiracy theories (such as the Illuminati supposedly controlling people's minds or a list of Bill and Hillary Clinton's alleged murders of supporters and acquaintances since the 1980s) or trade links to dubious conspiracy sites (such as Alex Jones' notorious InfoWars) while there is also the occasional anti-semitic "Jews control the media and the world" statement thrown in as well. Amidst the conspiracy clutter there are a few gems, such as the stories that rarely get reported in the mainstream media—especially the ones that take place in Asia, Africa, and the Middle East—along with some nice artwork and photography that have been uploaded by members. Minds is currently experimenting with giving its members the opportunity to earn money for posts (in the form of cryptocurrency) but I haven't heard of anyone actually making at least a decent part-time income yet. https://www.minds.com

Steemit is a social media site where members get paid for a post based on how many people read that post. It sounds great on the surface until you scroll down among the Trending articles and see that most of the people who are actually making money have earned no more than somewhere between 1-3 cents. (Yes, cents, not dollars.) While it's less busy compared to the more popular sites, Steemit does have its adherents and it may be worth your time to check it out. https://steemit.com/

Reddit is a social media site whose interface (which includes categories of reddits and subreddits) can be confusing for a newbie or a casual computer user who's used to Facebook, Twitter, or one of the other popular social media sites. Reddit is focused on having its members submit links and texts while other members will vote up or vote down a particular submission. https://www.reddit.com

Snapchat is a social media site that can only be accessed with a smartphone. The basic gist is that people will post a "moment" on Snapchat, which then disappears after 24 hours. This site has especially become very popular among teens. You can download the free Snapchat app from the App Store or Google Play.

Mastodon is an open source alternative to Twitter except it has a 500 character limit (versus Twitter's 280 characters). https://joinmastodon.org

Diaspora is an open source alternative to Facebook.
https://diasporafoundation.org

Free Online Entertainment

There are times when you simply want to sit down, relax, put your feet up, and watch something on the computer screen. It can be hard for a cash-strapped person to pay a monthly subscription fee for—let's say—Netflix or Amazon Prime. The good news is that there are free alternatives where you can just sit back, relax, and watch something interesting or play an online game.

YouTube (https://www.youtube.com) has recently started its YouTube Premium where, for a monthly fee, you can watch original series and movies made especially for that platform. But the good news is that there is still plenty of free content that you can watch without having to subscribe to its Premium service and new free content is being uploaded by users all the time. If you're in the mood for a feature length movie, the good news is that there are plenty of free movies on YouTube that you can legally watch without paying a single penny. For more details, check out the following links:

https://www.dailydot.com/upstream/free-movies-on-youtube-public-domain/

https://www.digitaltrends.com/movies/best-free-movies-on-youtube/

https://www.lifewire.com/best-free-movies-on-youtube-4159869

https://www.thrillist.com/entertainment/nation/youtube-free-movies

The Internet Archive has both movies and games you can watch or play for free. Check out this treasure trove of fun:

Classic MS-DOS games:
https://archive.org/details/softwarelibrary_msdos_games

Classic PC games:
https://archive.org/details/classicpcgames

The Internet Arcade:
https://archive.org/details/internetarcade

Moving Image Archive: https://archive.org/details/movies

Movies: https://archive.org/details/moviesandfilms

Open Culture has all a list of 1,150 free movies covering all kinds of genres:

http://www.openculture.com/freemoviesonline

Vimeo has a paid subscription program but it still has plenty of videos you can watch for free—with many of them in 4K Ultra HD. Many of the free videos are by aspiring filmmakers but you can find a few gems there. https://vimeo.com

Daily Motion is another site where you can watch videos for free. https://www.dailymotion.com/

LiveLeak is another site where you can watch videos for free. https://www.liveleak.com

DLive advertises itself as being the next generation live streaming and video community on the Blockchain. Like the other platforms, you can watch videos for free. https://dlive.io

Kanopy is an online streaming platform with 26,000 movies, documentaries, indie films, and foreign language films that one can access for free with a library card. For more information, ask your librarian.

Here's a situation. Let's say you're traveling somewhere and you want to watch a few videos while you're on the road but you're not sure if the place you're going to will have a reliable Internet connection or not. **ClipGrab** is a free app where you can download videos to your hard drive from YouTube, Facebook, Vimeo, and other social media sites so you can view them off-line later. https://clipgrab.org/

Free Recipes Online

There was a time when, if you wanted new recipes because you were tired of cooking the same old meals day after day, you had very few options. One was to have your parents or other relatives give you a copy of your favorite relative's recipe that you loved to eat every time you visited the family. Another was to go to a bookstore, look for a cookbook that grabs your eye, buy it, then use it to make some new meals.

Thanks to the Internet these days, getting family recipes from relatives or buying cookbooks have become passé. The one big advantage of doing your own online search is that you can get a new recipe for free immediately without buying a cookbook or waiting for your Aunt Martha to get around to giving you the recipe for her French onion soup that you've always loved.

Let's say you are in the mood for some chicken carbonara but you don't have a recipe All you have to do is do a Google search under "chicken carbonara" (without the quotation marks) and you'll get at least one recipe that will enable you to cook that chicken carbonara.

But let's say you are in the mood to cook something new but you aren't sure where to begin. Here are some websites that will provide some inspiration on what to cook next.

Genius Kitchen: https://www.geniuskitchen.com
Allrecipes: https://www.allrecipes.com
Epicurious: https://www.epicurious.com
SuperCook: https://www.supercook.com/
Disney Family Recipes: https://family.disney.com/recipes/
Food Network's Recipes:
https://www.foodnetwork.com/recipes

Free eBooks

While the public library has long been a place where the literary-minded cash-strapped could borrow a book for free, there are online places where you can download a variety of free eBooks to your computer, tablet or smartphone. Unlike a traditional library, you con't have to worry about returning these books within a certain timeframe or fret about paying fines for returning them past the due date.

The Internet Archive offers over 15,000,000 freely downloadable books and texts in a variety of genres. https://archive.org/details/texts

Open Library provides free books, many of which have fallen out of copyright and into the public domain.

https://openlibrary.org

Project Gutenberg offers over 57,000 free ebooks in a variety of genres. https://www.gutenberg.org

Read Print has thousands of online books you can read for free. http://www.readprint.com

Many Books have free ebooks available for your Kindle or other tablet. http://manybooks.net

If you prefer audiobooks to reading text, **LibriVox** has free public domain recordings made by volunteers located all over the world. https://librivox.org

Authorama focuses exclusively on public domain books, which are in the HTML format so you can read them in your web browser. http://www.authorama.com

Questia has over 5,000 public domain books for you to read, including some rare books. https://www.questia.com/library/free-books

Wikisource is another source of free public domain books. https://en.wikisource.org/wiki/Main_Page

Wikibooks have books that you can read for free. https://en.wikibooks.org/wiki/Main_Page

Free eBooks offers books written by all-new rising authors and independent writers for free. It's a good place to discover new talent. https://www.free-ebooks.net

The Online Books Page, which is maintained by the University of Pennsylvania, has a listing of over 2 million free

books for you to download.
http://digital.library.upenn.edu/books/

Free Sites For Online Dating or Just Meeting New People in General

Are you looking for love in all the wrong places? Looking for a platonic friend or two to do fun things like going shopping or playing golf? Are you the new person in town and you don't know where to begin for meeting and making new friends? Here are a few free resources you can use whether you're looking for a new friend, new lover, or both.

I've already written about **Meetup** as being the best place for networking with people who could help you in your job search. Meetup can also function as a place where you can meet new friends in general. All you have to do is conduct a search based on your favorite hobby or interest (such as a certain genre of books or playing video games or golfing or wine tasting). Chances are that there will be at least one group with your interest in mind (especially if you live in a well-populated area of the country). Sign up for that group then go out the next time that group announces an in-person meetup. Just remember to come up with a budget of how much money you can afford to spend if the group is meeting in a bar, restaurant, or cafe. https://www.meetup.com

Shapr is a free smartphone app that's been described as "Tinder for professionals." It has a similar interface to Tinder but instead of looking for a date, you are looking for people to meet in person and network with. When you first sign up you mention what you're interested in and Shapr will try to match you with people who share similar interests. Each day you are given a bunch of people's profiles to look through. If you like what you see in a certain person, you swipe right. If that person doesn't interest you in any way, you swipe left. Afterwards you can make arrangements with the other person to meet with you either online or in real life. Shapr can be downloaded for free from the App Store or Google Play.

Happied is a website where you can find the Happy Hour that's currently going on nearest to you. So far Washington, DC is only listed with other cities going online soon. https://www.happied.co

OKCupid is a dating site that's free to join, free to search, and free to message. It's also very LGBTQ friendly. https://www.okcupid.com/

Plenty Of Fish is another dating site that's free to use while looking for someone. https://www.pof.com

Tindr is a free dating app where, each day, you are given a bunch of people's profiles to look through. If you like what you see in a certain person, you swipe right. If that person doesn't interest you in any way, you swipe left. Tindr has long had a reputation of being more of a place for a one-night stand or a temporary hookup instead of finding everlasting love but if that's what you want, you can download it for free from the App Store or Google Play.

Hinge, which promotes itself as "thoughtful dating for thoughtful people," is more focused on finding someone to have a long-term relationship with. You can download it for free from the App Store or Google Play.

Pure is a free dating app for those who are looking for a discreet short-term affair. You can download it from the App Store or Google Play.

Grindr is a free dating app that's specifically for gay/bisexual/transgender men and it also has a reputation for being more of a hookup app than a place where you can find a long-term meaningful relationship. You can download it from the App Store or Google Play.

Her is a free dating app for lesbian/bisexual/transgender women. You can download it for free from the App Store or Google Play.

Coffee Meets Bagel is another free dating app that you can download from the App Store or Google Play.

Happn is an app for those romantics who believe in love at first site and are into the idea of meeting their true love for the first time in a public place. Happn uses your current location to alert you to other users nearby. If you're too shy to come up to a stranger, Happn will alert that other person that you're nearby and want to talk to that person. You can download it for free from the App Store or Google Play.

hater is a dating app with a twist. Instead of matching you with someone else who likes the same things you do, this site will match you with someone based on the fact that you hate the same thing. In other words, if you really hate—let's say—Donald Trump, hater will try to match you with a fellow Trump hater in the hopes that some bonding based on a mural hatred will happen. You can download it for free from the App Store or Google Play.

Exploring Your Spirituality

These days nearly every religious tradition has an Internet presence. You can easily learn more about a certain faith by doing a simple Google search.

But let's say you weren't raised in any particular faith as a child. Or you were brought up in a certain religion but you felt so alienated by that faith that you left it as an adult. Or the religious faith that you currently belong to hasn't been resonating much with you lately like it used to. In any case, you've been feeling an internal urge to consider exploring your own spirituality with other people in a setting that's away from the computer screen but you don't know where to begin.

In the pre-Internet days the solution would've been to attending various masses or services in a variety of houses of worship until you find something that you feel comfortable with. The big disadvantages are that this method was very time-consuming plus there are some religions that are big on proselytizing so once you appear at a service, these faiths would do everything possible to pressure you into joining even if you've decided that this particular faith isn't a good fit with you.

Belief-O-Matic is a free online quiz you can do in the comfort of your home that will help you find the religious tradition that's right for you. Basically you answer a series of 20 questions that probe where you personally stand on a variety of religious, spiritual, ethical, and moral issues. At the end of the quiz, Belief-O-Matic will come up with a list of 27 religious faiths that best suit you based on your own answers. Obviously the religions that are ranked higher on that list are the ones that are most likely to fit you. Once you take the quiz, the next step is for you to do Google searches about these faiths (I would personally advise you with sticking with just the top five faiths on your list) and if there are any local churches/mosques/synagogues/temples in your area where you can attend a religious service and get a feel for a certain

faith and the people who belong to it.
http://www.beliefnet.com/entertainment/quizzes/beliefomatic.as
px

The Internet Sacred Text Archive contains free books about religion, mythology, folklore, and the esoteric in general. This is a good resource if you want to explore your spirituality in the privacy of your home. http://www.sacred-texts.com

Support Your Local Library and STEM/STEAM Makerspace

Combination Library/STEM center in Savage, Maryland.

Throughout this book I've mentioned using your local public library and STEM/STEAM makerspace, both of which offer access to computers and other types of technology.

The public library frequently have free wi-fi for those who bring their laptops or smartphones so one can surf the Internet for free. If you didn't bring either, the library will frequently have computers on site that you can borrow for free. In addition, the public library has online goodies for its patrons ranging from music lessons to access to online classes through Lynda and Rosetta Stone to providing online job hunting advice—all of which can be accessed for free with a library card. (By the way, you can get a library card free as long as you have an ID.) This is definitely not your parents' (or even grandparents') library.

A makerspace is a communal place where people get together and make things using a variety of computers and other tools that are available. The makerspace focuses on STEM (which stands for **S**cience, **T**echnology, **E**ngineering, and **M**ath) while some also focuses on STEAM (the "A" stands for **A**rt). Some makerspaces are non-profit where a membership fee is either free or minimal while others are for-profit operations where membership fees are based on a variety of factors. There are even wide variations from makerspace to makerspace. Some makerspaces focuses more on children's activities, some may focus more on the arts and crafts end of STEAM, some may be geared more towards adults while providing training, some may focus more on the STEM end than the STEAM end, etc. It's not unusual to walk into a makerspace and see a girl working on her first robot using the LEGO Mindstorms kit while a man is using an electric saw to work on his woodworking project. Nearby two boys are playing Minecraft together while two women are sitting together chatting while they are working on their latest knitting project. More and more makerspaces are opening across the country, which can revolutionize the way that people work and socialize together.

If that's not enough, I've seen libraries that also function as makerspaces. Frequently the makerspace is located in a room or two where library patrons are free to use the facilities to make things. I've seen two such library-makerspace hybrids in Maryland (where I currently live)—one in Savage and the other in Rockville.

To find the library and/or makerspace that's near you, do a Google search on the following (without the quote marks): "public library near me" and "makerspace near me".

Only the educated are free.

Epictetus

Protecting Yourself Legally Without Spending Tons of Money on Legal Fees

All of the tips I provided in this book are legal. Just because they are legal today doesn't mean that they won't somehow become illegal sometime in the future. Even before the 2016 election of Donald Trump to the White House there have been increasing concerns about the rise of monopolies and a new class of oligarchs that could negatively impact civil liberties due in large part to changing or loosening of regulations that began under Ronald Reagan but has continued under both Democratic and Republican administrations alike. Here is a recent example.

President Donald Trump appointed a former Verizon executive named Ajit Pai as chairman of the Federal Communications Commission, who managed to succeed in his quest to do away with Net Neutrality (where Internet service providers and telecommunications companies are supposed to provide equal online access to everyone), which benefits his former company. With the repeal of Net Neutrality, those who provide access to the Internet are free to throttle access to certain websites unless those sites can pay a large monthly fee to those companies. Naturally sites with the financial backing of large corporations will be able to afford to pay those fees more than sites with tighter budgets, such as small locally-owned businesses, nonprofits, and local government agencies. (https://www.nytimes.com/2017/11/29/technology/internet-dying-repeal-net-neutrality.html)

The landmark *Citizens United v. FEC* Supreme Court case (https://en.wikipedia.org/wiki/Citizens_United_v._FEC) has only exacerbated the situation where this society has increasingly experienced a wider gap between the 1% of the population who has all the power and material goods (including access to the latest computers with fastest Internet speeds and high-end software) and the 99% who have far less.

This rise in income inequality affecting civil liberties has even spilled over into computers and high tech. In 2018 a man in California named Eric Lundgren was sentenced to serve 15 months in prison. His crime? He attempted to recycle computers using restore discs containing the Microsoft Windows operating system which he copied himself. (http://www.latimes.com/business/technology/la-fi-tn-microsoft-copyright-20180426-story.html) What's even more outrageous is that Lundgren was sentenced to serve more time in prison than another California man named Brock Turner, who was actually caught in the very act of raping a woman who had passed out from consuming too much alcohol. He was sentenced to serve only six months in prison but ended up being released after serving just three months. (https://www.nytimes.com/2018/08/09/us/brock-turner-appeal.html)

That's right, the state of California has decided that getting justice on behalf of Microsoft is far more important than getting justice on behalf of a rape victim.

With a lopsided system like that, it has become more imperative to educate yourself on how you can legally defend yourself despite being on a very tight budget. Even if you're not concerned about civil rights at the moment, there are times when you may need to use the legal system for things like getting a divorce, child custody issues, dealing with an employer who haven't been paying you for work you have already done, etc. Here are some places to go where you can get legal advice and maybe even a lawyer who's willing to either work pro bono or won't charge you any money unless you win a huge cash award by a court.

Stateside Legal has links to state and local organizations that low-income individuals can tap into. https://statesidelegal.org/lso

Flikshop has a service where, for as low as 79 cents, you can send photos from your phone, Facebook, or Instagram that are printed on a 4" x 6" postcard to an incarcerated friend or loved one. http://www.flikshop.com

The American Civil Liberties Union (ACLU) has long fought on behalf of civil liberties on a variety of issues while taking many of these cases pro-bono. The ACLU also has a Mobile Justice smartphone app that you can download for free from the App Store or Google Play. (Each Mobile Justice app is specified to a particular state so download the app that represents where you live or where you currently are located at the moment.) If you see any acts of police brutality or some other kind of incidents that could potentially threaten civil liberties, all you have to do is to load the app, shoot a video through that app, then press a button that will immediately send that video to a local ACLU chapter. https://www.aclu.org/

Reyets is an app for journalists, activists, and others to record and document any abuses that go on by people in positions of authorities which also has a community feature where you can contact an collaborate with other like-minded people as well as a feature where you can know your legal rights with the touch of a screen. https://www.reyets.com

DoNotPay is an iPhone app which helps you with filing a lawsuit without hiring a lawyer first. https://www.donotpay.com/

Shortcuts is an iPhone-only app where you can put together a script featuring a variety of different apps that your phone can activate at the proper moment. This article shows how you can use it in case you get pulled over by the police. https://www.businessinsider.com/ios-12-shortcut-uses-iphone-to-record-police-during-traffic-stop-2018-10

Electronics Freedom Foundation (EFF) is dedicated to defending civil liberties online, including restoring Net Neutrality in the United States, preserving rights to privacy while online, and providing government transparency. https://www.eff.org/

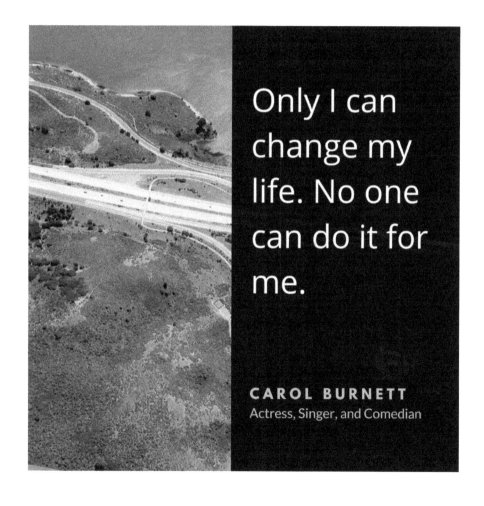

Only I can change my life. No one can do it for me.

CAROL BURNETT
Actress, Singer, and Comedian

Other Free Resources

Free Free FREE

Free Free

FREE Free

Free Free

Free FREE

Free

This book only scratches the surface of the things you can get online for free. For those who want to delve deeper into this, here are a few sites you can check out.

The Free Site has been online since the 1990s but it's still an amazing resource for free things you can get, ranging from free web hosting services to free internet access to free apps you can get from your tablet or smartphone. The Free Site is updated on a regular basis with new things that one can legally get for free online. This site has even expanded its lists of freebies to include non-technical freebies, such as where to find free food or household items. https://www.thefreesite.com

OpenSource.com covers just about everything to do with free open source software ranging from open source alternatives to Skype to the best open source racing and flying games for Linux. If you are a programmer or if you are into information technology (IT) in general, this site has all kinds of technical articles you can sink your teeth into. https://opensource.com/

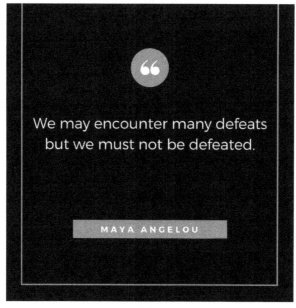

> We may encounter many defeats but we must not be defeated.
>
> MAYA ANGELOU

In Conclusion

I'm going to tell you a brief story about a boy named William Kamkwamba who grew up in poverty in Malawi. He initially went to school until he was forced to drop out at 14 when his parents could no longer afford to pay his tuition fee. In a desperate attempt to retain his education, he started to visit the village library on a regular basis. When he discovered a book in the library called Using Energy, he got the idea to create a makeshift wind turbine that would provide electricity to his village. He built this wind turbine using recycled materials like bicycle parts and plastic pipes.

The wind turbine was a success and William Kamkwamba began to get attention from around the world. He later became the subject of a book called *The Boy Who Harnessed the Wind*.

If you were to look at the high tech companies in the United States, you'll see that since the rise of the information superhighway in the 1990s, they have been dominated by white heterosexual men who came from upper class backgrounds and who attended Ivy League or other expensive name brand schools (like Stanford). If you look at the companies based in high tech areas like Silicon Valley or New York City or Northern Virginia, it's the same situation.

This lack of diversity in high tech has created problems, such as the numerous controversies surrounding Uber (https://www.recode.net/2018/2/5/16777536/uber-travis-kalanick-recruit-drivers-tipping), the number of powerful high tech people who have been accused of sexual harassment or misconduct (https://www.businessinsider.com/biggest-tech-scandals-2017-12#june-through-december-several-powerful-investors-bloggers-and-ceos-are-accused-of-sexual-harassment-or-misconduct-6), and how many of these tech companies have developed a bro culture that's similar to a college fraternity house and it also excludes women and people of color. (On that note, I highly recommend reading Emily Chang's book *Brotopia*, which documents how women have been systematically shut out of Silicon Valley, and Safiya Noble's *Algorithms of Oppression*, which shows how algorithms programmed by white males reinforce racism. Cash-strapped people can easily find these books in your local public library or even a used book store.)

Think about how the landscape would be different if other types of people were allowed to work in high tech. These people could provide perspectives that are different from the white bro culture. Think about the innovations that could result from having a more diverse group of people who could collaborate with each other—innovations that would be just as mind-blowing as William Kamkwamba's homemade wind turbine. Every time there are barriers to having different groups of people getting involved in high tech (whether it's financial or otherwise), that's another potential for innovation that remains untapped. Imagine what life would be like today had—let's say—Jonas Salk been denied the chance to go to medical school or even higher education in general after high school. There's a big possibility that polio would still be a problem today.

With this book I hope I have inspired you to get involved in high tech making do with what you currently have. Who knows? Maybe one day a person who reads this book will use this information to invent something extraordinary that benefits humankind.

In this book I've managed to give you the information that you can use to improve your life and change it for the better. Now the rest is up to you. It's time for you to get to work and turn your dreams into a reality.

A Special Treat For Those Who Have Read This Book

No, Zombie Dog, that's not what I meant!

Whether you've read this book all the way through to this page or you're just skimming through the book and you happen to find this page, I have to say congratulations for trying this book. I would suggest treating yourself to a meal at a nice restaurant but the problem is that eating out can be so expensive these days, especially if you're a cash-strapped person. (I've even seen meals at certain fast food restaurants total around $10.) As a special thank you for buying and reading this book, I'm going to give you something that you can use to treat yourself and your family without breaking your personal bank account.

One of this book's inspirations came from Abbie Hoffman's *Steal This Book*. Among that book's tips on obtaining free or low-cost food, clothing, housing, medical care, etc. are a few recipes that Hoffman called "Cheap Chow" because the ingredients were relatively inexpensive to obtain. You can download a free copy of *Steal This Book*, including the Cheap Chow recipes, from the Internet Archive. (https://archive.org/details/pdfy-TNIDHryRIk4DXKAU)

I have a few free recipes of my own where the ingredients are relatively cheap to obtain and it provides enough food to feed an average family. If you have any leftovers, they will freeze really well.

I know some of you reading this will question whether including a recipe in a book that's mostly about high tech is even appropriate. Granted this is unusual but it's not unprecedented. In the book written by Joelle Reeder and Katherine Scoleri, *The IT Girl's Guide to Blogging With Moxie*, there were recipes for various drinks that were placed at the end of each chapter, which discussed the various aspects of blogging.

The first recipe is for corn chowder and it's one that is not only easy and inexpensive to make but there's a story behind it, which makes it sentimental for me.

My future ex-husband grew up on Long Island with his two siblings. His parents became close friends with another couple named Annette and Joe, who also had three children. Annette and Joe started a holiday tradition where each Christmas Eve they would invite my future in-laws and their children over to their home for dinner where Annette would serve her corn chowder along with a variety of breads and side dishes. After dinner the kids would play board games while the adults socialized. At one point Annette would play her piano while everyone sang Christmas carols. The party ended when Annette and Joe would gather their children so they could attend midnight mass at a local Catholic church while my in-laws and their kids returned to their home.

The first change in that annual tradition came after my husband and his siblings became young adults and my in-laws got a divorce. My future father-in-law converted to Orthodox Judaism shortly before he married his second wife. In accordance with the requirements of his new faith, he could no longer observe Christmas nor eat corn chowder (even if the corn chowder had been made with all-beef hot dogs instead of kielbasa or knackwurst, it would've violated the Jewish law against mixing meat and dairy products). In fact, he could no longer eat anything that was made in Annette and Joe's kitchen because it wasn't kosher certified. (Despite the drastic change in his beliefs and lifestyle, he managed to stay with both his wife and his faith until his death in 2017.)

After the divorce Annette and Joe continued to invite my mother-in-law over to their place for dinner on Christmas Eve while extending that invitation to any of her adult children who happened to be in town at the moment. When my relationship with my then-boyfriend became serious to the point where we were starting to discuss marriage, he took me to his mother's place (she was living in Yonkers at the time) where the three of us traveled to Annette and Joe's home on Long Island and I tried Annette's corn chowder for the first time. I loved that dish and I also loved the tradition where the family members and guests played board games and socialized. I still remember Annette playing Christmas songs on her piano that was in the living room.

After I got married we continued that tradition of eating corn chowder at Annette and Joe's place for a few more years where I loved it each time. That annual tradition abruptly ended one year when Annette and Joe's own marriage collapsed and they got a divorce. My husband and I would see Joe only once after the divorce and that was at the wedding of one of his children. (Joe passed away in 2009.) We would continue to see Annette from time to time but she had discontinued the Christmas Eve get-togethers.

My mother-in-law decided to step up and continue the tradition of serving corn chowder on Christmas Eve so she managed to get Annette to give her a copy of the recipe. My mother-in-law would serve the corn chowder in her Yonkers condo for anyone who was visiting on Christmas Eve for a few more years. When she remarried, she decided to move to her new husband's hometown of Phoenix. She continued to serve corn chowder on Christmas Eve to her husband and any members of their extended family who happened to be at the house. (My ex-husband's step-father, who passed away in 2018, had four children from a previous marriage, all of whom lived in the Phoenix metropolitan area with their spouses and children.)

At that point my husband and I weren't able to travel to Phoenix each Christmas (we did it some years but we couldn't afford to do it each year) so he asked his mother for a copy of the recipe and she gave it to us. I started to cook corn chowder for the two of us each Christmas Eve. There were other times of the year when I cooked corn chowder because I found the recipe so easy to make and the ingredients were inexpensive. My husband never seemed to mind eating corn chowder in the spring or fall in addition to eating it on Christmas Eve.

My mother-in-law continued the tradition of making corn chowder each Christmas Eve until her death in 2010. I continued making corn chowder each Christmas Eve even after my own marriage ended when my husband walked out on me just three days after Christmas in 2011. (Heck, my husband left just days after I cooked what turned out to be the last Christmas Eve corn chowder I ever made for him.) The reason why I continued to make the corn chowder each Christmas Eve is because I like the recipe, it's easy to make, the ingredients are inexpensive, and I can freeze the leftovers to eat later. Making it is also more poignant for me because Annette, the woman who introduced this meal to me, passed away in 2017.

Corn Chowder Recipe

1/2 cup chopped onions
1/2 cup chopped celery
1 lb. of either knackwurst, kielbasa, or hot dogs
1 1 lb. can cream-style corn
2 12 oz. cans whole kernel corn
1 tsp. salt (which can be omitted if you need to watch your salt intake)
1 cup milk (either whole or skim)
1/2 tsp. pepper
3 small potatoes, cubed
2 cups chicken broth or 2 cups boiling water mixed with two cubes chicken bouillon
1 1 lb. can tomatoes (optional)

Cut up the meat into smaller pieces and brown in pan. Mix the meat and the other ingredients into a pot and simmer on low heat on the stovetop for anywhere between 45 minutes-1 hour. Serves 4-6.

Here's a side dish that goes well with the corn chowder. There's no story behind this dish other than I found it in a recipe book a few years back. Like the corn chowder, this one is both easy and inexpensive to make and it's very tasty.

Asian-Style Green Beans

1 1 lb. bag of frozen green beans
2 Tbsp. sesame oil
4 Tbsp. soy sauce

Put the sesame oil in a pan or wok and heat on low to medium heat. Add the frozen green beans and the soy sauce. Heat for about 5-10 minutes while stirring every few minutes until the green beans are completely defrosted. Serves 4-6.

Sometimes there may be a special occasion where you may feel the need to have dessert. Here's a recipe that came from my mother. It was originally published in a late 1950's Betty Crocker cookbook that my father gave to my mother as a special present shortly after they were engaged (while sending a not-so-subtle hint that she needed to learn how to cook as soon as possible). The recipe was originally called "Black Midnight Cake" but there's a variation where you can drizzle hot fudge on top of the cake that my mother always made, which she called Hot Fudge Cake. I once made that cake for a town fair that earned me a third place ribbon in the Baked Goods-Cakes category. This cake is pretty easy to make and it's way cheaper than ordering something like this in a bakery.

Hot Fudge Cake

Buy the hot fudge sundae sauce. Put it aside while you focus on making the main part of the cake.

Cake Recipe

2/3 cup soft shortening
1 1/3 cup sugar
3 eggs
2 1/4 cups Softasilk Cake Flour
2/3 cup cocoa powder
1/4 teaspoon baking powder
1 1/4 teaspoon baking soda
1 1/3 cups water
1 teaspoon vanilla extract

Preheat oven at 350 degrees. Grease and flower either two 9" layer pans (for a layered cake) or one 13" x 9" oblong pan (for a larger single layer cake). Mix all of the ingredients together in a mixing bowl. Pour the mix into the baking pan(s) and bake at 350 degrees for either 35 minutes (for the 9" layer pans) or 40-45 minutes (for the 13" x 9" oblong pan). After baking let it sit for about 10-15 minutes the remove from the pan(s). Place on a plate or a cooling rack and let cake cool completely before frosting.

White Frosting Recipe**

2 egg whites
1 teaspoon vanilla extract
1/2 cup sugar
2 tablespoons water
1/4 cup light corn syrup

Mix sugar, water, and corn syrup in a saucepan and bring it to boil over the stovetop. Add the egg whites and continue to beat until the frosting hold peaks. Blend in the vanilla extract.

About the Author

Kimberly Keyes was born in Baltimore and grew up in nearby Glen Burnie, Maryland. She holds a Bachelor's of Science degree in Journalism from the University of Maryland at College Park and she has written articles for a variety of publications as varied as OpenSource.com and *The Greenbelt News Review*. She currently lives outside of Washington, DC. She can be reached via email at kimberlyannkeyes@gmail.com and online at the following:

Blog: https://sagittariusdolly.wordpress.com

Website: https://sagittariusdolly.neocities.org

Twitter: https://twitter.com/funkyartist

Facebook: https://www.facebook.com/KimberlyKeyesArtist/

Instagram: https://www.instagram.com/kimberlyannkeyes/

Sagittarius Dolly YouTube Channel:
https://www.youtube.com/channel/UC4jg0FNKm_CLu0MqlMd_6aw/videos

Twisted Unicorn YouTube Channel:
https://www.youtube.com/user/twistedunicorn/videos

Kim Keyes screencasts YouTube Channel:
https://www.youtube.com/channel/UC4ktX8w10xVIZ95v-3471tg/videos

LinkedIn: https://www.linkedin.com/in/kimberlyannkeyes/

Jobcase: https://www.jobcase.com/p/kimberly.keyes18

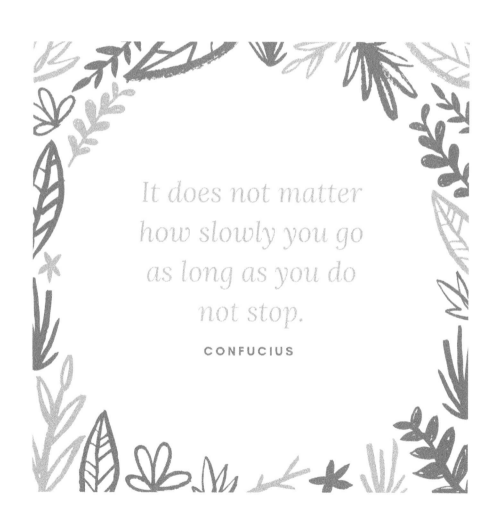